The Observers Series
FLAGS

About the Book

More and more people of all ages are becoming interested in flags, particularly national flags, and would like to know about their symbolism and the factors influencing their design. New nations are coming into existence—over eighty since the Second World War—with flag designs that may seem strange and baffling.

The new edition of this popular book—thoroughly revised, enlarged and brought up to date—introduces the reader to the flags of all nations, the old as well as the new, and illustrates them with many colour pictures and line drawings. There is also a section on international flags.

American and UK flags and their historical development are described in separate sections, and no country is neglected in the exhaustive A to Z of Nations.

About the Author

Besides being an organizer and tutor in adult education, William Crampton is the Director of the Flag Institute, a body of researchers and associates interested in all aspects of flags. He has had a lifelong fascination for flags and has built up a collection of data which is probably unrivalled in Britain. He also designs flags, particularly for regional and civic use, and his work can be seen in the flags of a number of the new local government areas.

He collaborated with Captain E.M.C. Barraclough on the 1978 edition of *Flags of the World* (updated 1981), a standard work on the subject, and is also the author of a number of booklets on flag design and flag etiquette.

The *Observer's* series was launched in 1937 with the publication of *The Observer's Book of Birds*. Today, fifty years later, paperback *Observers* continue to offer practical, useful information on a wide range of subjects, and with every book regularly revised by experts, the facts are right up-to-date. Students, amateur enthusiasts and professional organisations alike will find the latest *Observers* invaluable.

'Thick and glossy, briskly informative' – *The Guardian*

'If you are a serious spotter of any of the things the series deals with, the books must be indispensable' – *The Times Educational Supplement*

929

FLAGS

William G. Crampton

FREDERICK WARNE

FREDERICK WARNE

Published by the Penguin Group
27 Wrights Lane, London W8 5TZ, England
Viking Penguin Inc., 40 West 23rd Street, New York, New York 10010, USA
Penguin Books Australia Ltd, Ringwood, Victoria, Australia
Penguin Books Canada Ltd, 2801 John Street, Markham, Ontario, Canada L3R 1B4
Penguin Books (NZ) Ltd, 182–190 Wairau Road, Auckland 10, New Zealand

Penguin Books Ltd, Registered Offices: Harmondsworth, Middlesex, England

First published 1959
New edition 1979
Reprinted with revisions 1986, 1988

Copyright © Frederick Warne & Co., 1979, 1986, 1988

Originally published as *The Observer's Book of Flags*
in small hardback format.

ISBN 0 7232 1667 3

Printed and bound in Great Britain by
William Clowes Limited, Beccles and London

CONTENTS

PREFACE

The serious study of flags is one of the newest pursuits available to those who take an intelligent interest in the world around them. It is a bit like ornithology in that it involves 'spotting', identification, classification, and some knowledge of backgrounds, types, and various features and their functions. It is also a bit like history, in that it includes some understanding of past events and how they came about, and a bit like geography in that the flag student has to know his way around the world (from the depths of an armchair), and to learn the locations of some very obscure places. Its nearest relatives are the collection of stamps and coins, and heraldry. Unlike the devotee of stamps and coins, the flag student does not usually collect actual flags, but only information about them. He relies on books such as this one for facts and illustrations, but he will also be on the alert for flags flying anywhere, particularly in the countries he is interested in. This makes flag study an especially rewarding occupation for those who travel abroad, since strange flags are among the first objects to greet the eye. Like stamp collectors, flag enthusiasts often specialize in themes, such as the flags of football clubs, shipping lines, airlines, cities and regions, rather than trying to take in the entire range of flags of a particular country. They may also specialize in particular periods of history, for instance Napoleonic times, the English Civil Wars, the Second World War. In this way flag students are related to those interested in war games and military modelling, who are also enthusiasts with a keen sense of historical background, and a great deal of information passes backwards and forwards between the two groups. Flags, especially those which are heraldic in origin, or which are complicated and detailed, are also a field of interest for those with artistic inclinations, since they offer many challenging opportunities for painting and drawing.

In a world where international trade and contacts of all kinds are rapidly increasing it is impossible to go for long without a knowledge of the flags of other countries. This knowledge needs to be kept constantly up to date, since national flags can be changed quite frequently, as countries become independent or as their governments change. This can happen in any part of the world, and embarrassing incidents could occur, particularly in diplomatic or commercial circles, if obsolete flags were employed. A handbook of this sort can keep the reader almost up to date, and frequent revisions will help, but it does need to be borne in mind that events can often overtake printing.

Those interested in flags will find that they are among a great many in most advanced countries of the world who have taken up this interest. There are now clubs and societies in most countries of Europe, as well as in the USA and Japan, which are bound together in an international federation. The previous editor of this book, I. O. Evans, was a keen promoter of this activity and did a lot to establish the Flag Institute in Britain, and to make flag study an accepted pursuit with high standards of accuracy and always abreast of current developments. This edition will attempt to keep up to these high standards.

W. G. C.

Note. Figures in the margins refer to colour illustrations.

INTRODUCTION

Flags have played an important part in human life since the beginnings of recorded history. Archaeology has revealed their use in the Iran of five thousand years ago, in Egypt from the First Dynasty, and in ancient China. In these early days 'flags' were solid objects on poles, although often with coloured ribbons attached. The earliest flags of a modern kind were the Roman *vexilla* (from which the name of the science of flags, 'vexillology', is derived), and the *draco* standards. The *vexillum* was a square of cloth hung from a horizontal cross-bar, a form still in use today. The *draco* was a hollow cloth tube in the shape of a dragon, designed to inflate in the wind. This principle was also used in the 'Raven', the standard of the Vikings, whilst the *Labarum*, the later Roman standard, was based on the *vexillum*.

Designs on cloth, usually in the form of inscriptions, came in with the Arab conquests. Designs in the form of heraldic devices developed when the Crusades were launched. In Christian lands crosses were the earliest emblems used by those fighting the tide of Islam, and these came to be worn on surcoats, shields, and eventually on flags. From such simple devices are derived the flags of England, Scotland, Denmark, and medieval France.

Heraldry regularized and codified the growing mass of personal symbolism, and drew up rules for the depiction and use of a coat of arms. One of these uses was on a **banner** consisting of the arms spread over a rectangular cloth. A modern example of such a flag is the armorial banner of the late Sir Winston Churchill. Another way of using the arms was on a standard, which came to mean a cloth coloured according to the bearer's livery, and charged with (carrying) one or more of his badges. From a standard of this kind is derived the flag of

1 *A banner of arms:
the late Sir Winston
Churchill*

2 *Banner
of England*

3 *Banner
of Scotland*

4 *UK:
present royal
standard*

5 *UK: Queen's
personal flag*

6 *HRH Prince
Philip, Duke of
Edinburgh's standard*

11

Wales. Military **colours** are also derived from medieval heraldic standards, but are outside the scope of this book.

Until modern times few flags represented a distinct nation, as opposed to a feudal lordship, a religion, or a military unit. In medieval England it was uncertain for a long time what represented the nation: the royal arms or the cross of St George. But eventually the royal arms came to represent the king alone, and the cross of St George the people and thereby the nation. A similar process took place in Scotland, France, and Denmark. In other parts of Europe city flags, such as those of Hamburg, Genoa and Venice, emerged as the first truly national flags. They had simple designs easily recognizable at sea when used by the merchant ships of these city states. Modern national flags are often a combination of the heraldic and maritime trends.

In modern times colours in themselves, or more usually groups of colours such as red, white, and blue, have taken on a particular political significance. Many countries with flags of two colours, or of three colours (tricolours) have adopted them to signify a political or national affiliation. The flag of the Netherlands was probably the first national flag of this kind, and it was copied with variations by Russia and later by many other countries. Thus the flags of Yugoslavia and Czechoslovakia signify their affiliation to the Pan-Slav movement initiated in Russia. In South America, Argentina and Uruguay share colours which signify their liberation, as do Venezuela, Colombia and Ecuador. In Africa, red, yellow, and green have become known as the Pan-African colours, since so many countries, starting with Ghana in 1957, have adopted them. Elsewhere, black, red, and green, known as the Black Liberation colours, have come into widespread use. In Arab lands red, white, black and green have been almost universally adopted. These colours are thought to signify the whole spirit of modern Arabism. Red flags are now associated with communist countries, but not all communist countries employ them.

KINDS OF FLAGS

Flags have many forms, aside from the heraldic ones mentioned above. Every country has a **national flag**, now seen as the prime expression of national identity, and the supreme mark of independence. The hoisting of a national flag is almost always the symbol of the achievement of independence, a familiar procedure in recent years. Such a flag is for general use by the citizens, although often subject to a code of etiquette. In Britain this flag is the Union Jack, although unlike many countries Britain has never officially adopted a national flag. This shows that a national flag can be established by custom and tradition, as well as by a clause in a written constitution.

Many countries, particularly those in the British Commonwealth, have a distinctive flag for use on civil ships, known as the **civil flag** or **ensign**. This is often a simplified form of the national flag, but in the Commonwealth it is often based on the British merchant marine ensign, the Red Ensign.   16

The flag for use by naval vessels is called simply the **ensign**. In Britain this is the White Ensign, and ensigns based on this are 17 also used in many Commonwealth countries. Others often use an elaborated form of their national flag. Some countries have a distinctive flag for their air forces, known as the **air force ensign**, and even for use at civil air establishments, the **civil air ensign**. Many countries have a special **standard** for their Head of State, and those which are still monarchies have a **royal standard** (or indeed more than one, to cater for the various members of the royal family). Britain is now the only country to employ truly armorial banners for this purpose. Other countries do use heraldic emblems, but often in the form of embellished versions of the national flag or ensign. Such standards were originally and primarily for use afloat, but are now used in a variety of circumstances. One country, Israel, has a special form of the Presidential standard for use afloat.

Finally, one should mention the **jack**, a flag used in the bows of warships (and originally of merchant ships also). In Britain it

7 Prince of Wales' standard

8 HRH Prince Charles: flag for Wales

9 HRH Prince Charles: flag for Scotland

10 HM Queen Elizabeth the Queen Mother

14

*11   HRH
Princess Anne*

*12   England:
Cross of St George*

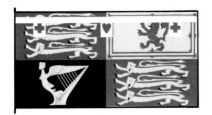

*13   Scotland:
Cross of St Andrew*

14   First Union Jack, 1606

is the Union Jack. Many countries use a flag with historical associations for this purpose, for instance the Irish Green Flag (see p. 120).

WHO USES FLAGS?

This question scarcely needs a reply, since the answer is evident all around us. Certainly national flags are the most obvious, due to the emancipation of so many nations involved in the dismantling of the empires of pre-1914 and the great colonial empires (to say nothing of the dozens of countries which have tried unsuccessfully to secure permanent independence in this century). However, in addition to this, flags are being employed on a wider scale than ever before by groups and institutions of all kinds. One of the most flag conscious countries in the world is Switzerland, and there it will be found that every place, from tiny commune to canton, including every village, town and city, has its own flag. This is also true in West Germany and the Netherlands, and to a lesser extent in many other European countries. Ethnic groups who are trying to establish a national identity also have them, such as the Basques, the Bretons, the Normans, and the Friesians, and many others whose flags can readily be spotted by the alert traveller. There is even a world gypsy flag!

Political parties in many countries have flags, although there is hardly any tradition of party flags in Britain. On the other hand Britain has a great many flags for commercial organizations, shipping and air lines, and for recreational clubs (but not for football clubs, although these too can be found in other countries). Clubs of all kinds, churches, universities, schools, colleges and all kinds of institutions are sporting flags in greater profusion than ever before. In the following pages predominance is given to national flags because space is restricted, and because such flags form the basis of others. But the reader should not feel that the subject has been exhausted with these alone.

FLAG TERMINOLOGY

In illustrations flags are normally shown as flying from the observer's left to his right, a view known as the **obverse**. However, as in heraldry, flags are always described in terms which express the view of the person holding them. Birds and beasts are, or should be, shown with their heads facing the flagstaff side, so that they are advancing, not running away, when a flag is carried along. This side is known as the **hoist**, and is to be understood as the half of the flag nearest the staff. The outer half is the **fly**. A flag is notionally divided into four quarters, called **cantons**, of which the upper hoist canton is known simply as **the canton**. Modern flags usually come from the manufacturer with a **hoist rope** sewn into the **sleeve.** At

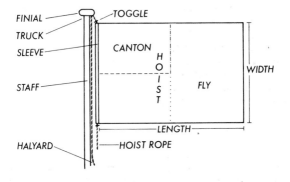

The parts of the flag and the flagstaff

the top of this is a **toggle** which fits into a loop or **becket** in the **halyards**. This tells one instantly if the flag is the right way up, but even so people seem to succeed in getting the Union Jack the wrong way up more often than is statistically probable.

17

*15 Present
Union Jack*

16 The Red Ensign

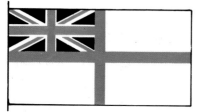

*17 The White
Ensign*

18 The Blue Ensign

19   UK: Chief of
Defence Staff

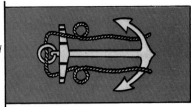

20   UK: Lord
High Admiral

21   UK:
Army ensign

22   UK:
RAF ensign

Modern flags are nearly always rectangular and oblong. Square flags are often found to be armorial banners, and longer flags are usually derived from maritime usage, as with the Union Jack. The oblong clearly preferred by the majority of flag users is the one with a ratio of width to length of 2:3, closely followed by 3:5 and 1:2, although almost every proportion in between can be found. The longest flag in the world is that of Iran, which is officially 1:3, as was that of Poland at one time. This proportion is more suitable, in practical terms, for flags meant to hang vertically, such as are often seen in Germany. Within the oblong shape a number of variations are possible, such as cutting a triangle out of the fly, to make a **swallow-tail**. It is also possible to make a **double swallow-tail** by leaving in a tongue of cloth: a form popular in northern Europe. Flags can also be embellished with fringes, and have accessories such as **cravats** (broad ribbons) attached below the **finial** (the top of the flagstaff, often itself made into an ornamental or symbolic shape).

Triangular shapes are usually reserved for flags of lesser importance than the oblong flag. This is exemplified in naval or other rank flags, where the high officers have oblong flags and the lesser ones triangular flags. Such flags are known as **pennons** or **pendants** regardless of how long they are. They too can be swallow-tailed, a form known in Britain as the **broad pendant**. Long pennons in the national colours were once attached to the lances of cavalry regiments, and still have a number of military functions today. The cravats mentioned above are descendants of the pennons often flown above a flag in bygone days, a practice still followed in the Netherlands, where an orange pennon is frequently added above the national flag. Long pendants are often flown from the mainmast of a warship to show it is in commission, and are therefore known as **commission pendants**. Similar flags can be used on commercial ships and yachts. The triangular flags used on yachts are called **burgees**.

FLAG ETIQUETTE

Care has to be used when displaying flags not to cause offence by disrespectful treatment. A prime rule is that no flag should be hoisted on the same halyard beneath another one: this symbolizes conquest and capture. In fact most of the points of etiquette involve the use of two or more flags together, and anyone proposing to do this is recommended to obtain specialist advice. It is also essential to get a flag the right way up: displayed upside down it signifies surrender, and in some cases it could turn into the flag of another country. It is also considered disrespectful to allow a flag to touch the ground, and lowering colours to the ground is a mark of signal respect to a Head of State. In Britain it has now been established beyond a doubt that the national flag, the Union Jack, may be freely displayed by all citizens, as for example during the 1977 Royal Jubilee. This is not the case with all national flags, however. In many European countries it is considered wrong to leave a flagstaff without a flag, also a sign of surrender! This is avoided by having a long pennant of the national colours hoisted when the flag is not flying. All countries have special days when flags must be flown, especially from public buildings. In Britain a list of days for flying the Union Jack may be obtained from the Department of the Environment, and there is also provision for flying the flags of Scotland and Wales. Flag etiquette is very important at sea, and often has the force of law. Naval vessels, civil ships, and yachts, are all covered in specialized hand-books.

A rule often transgressed by football supporters is that inscriptions or other additions may not be made to the national flag. Flags such as the Red and Blue Ensigns can have badges added, but only by special warrant. At sea, no flag may be displayed which looks like the national colours of any country, and national colours must be displayed when challenged. On the other hand any other flags may be flown in addition, such as a club burgee or owner's (or 'racing') flag.

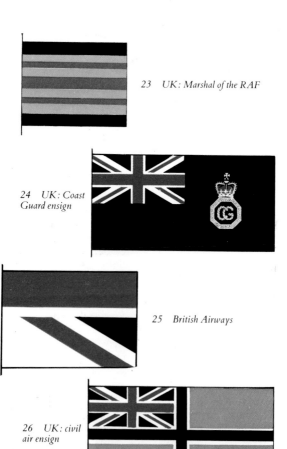

23 UK: Marshal of the RAF

24 UK: Coast Guard ensign

25 British Airways

26 UK: civil air ensign

27   British Rail

28   Wales: the
Red Dragon

29   Northern
Ireland

30   Isle of Man

A number of rules exist for achieving reasonable and meaningful designs for flags, and this is also an area where specialist advice is required. Those interested are recommended to contact the Flag Institute in Britain, or a similar organization in their own country.

THE UNITED KINGDOM

ROYAL STANDARDS

The royal standard of the United Kingdom is the armorial banner of the monarch and is inherited with the throne. Its quarters denote the three kingdoms over which the monarch has or has had dominion: England, Scotland, and Ireland. The arms of **England** were adopted in the reign of Richard I, and the Red Lion of **Scotland** appeared in 1165 in the reign of William the Lion. Its unusual border, known as a 'double treasure flory counterflory' and derived from the lilies of France, was added in 1222 during the reign of his son, Alexander II, to mark an association with France (the 'Auld Alliance'). The arms of Ireland derive from a badge known since Tudor times, being based on the famous harp of Brian Ború, first effective king of all Ireland.

The three arms were first 'marshalled' together in 1603 on the accession of James I. At that time they also included the three lilies of France, and these were not omitted until 1802. The present pattern dates from the accession of Queen Victoria in 1837. The banner is usually made in the proportions 1:2 in modern times, due to its prime use as a sea flag, but it was originally more nearly square, or even, in medieval times, twice as broad as long.

Wales was never a united state with arms of its own, and does not figure in the monarch's 'arms of dominion', although there are arms for the Prince of Wales.

The Queen also has a personal standard, somewhat similar to those used in medieval times, distinct from the royal banner. It was adopted in 1960 before her state visit to India and signifies her position as Head of the Commonwealth, rather than as Queen of a particular country. Corresponding royal flags have

31 *Jersey*

32 *Guernsey*

33 *Guernsey*

34 *Anguilla*

35 *Bermuda:*
ensign badge

36 *Cayman Islands:*
arms

37 *Falkland Islands:*
arms

been adopted for use in those Commonwealth countries which are not republics.

6 Prince Philip, Duke of Edinburgh, has a standard, flown everywhere in his presence, except when that of the Queen takes precedence. His standard quarters the arms of the families from which he is descended—the royal families of Denmark and Greece, and the Mountbattens—with the arms of the city of Edinburgh.

7 Prince Charles has three standards: one as Prince of Wales, which is the Royal Standard with a 'label', and an inescutcheon (a small central shield) of the arms of Wales. He also has a
8 personal flag for Wales, which is a square banner of the arms with a green inescutcheon bearing a princely coronet. For
9 Scotland he has another personal flag, with quarters for his Scottish titles. The quarters are: first and fourth, Stewart (for Great Steward of Scotland), second and third, Lord of the Isles; and on an inescutcheon are the arms of Rothesay.

10 The standard of Queen Elizabeth the Queen Mother is an example of an 'impaled' coat of arms of the kind used by the wife of a reigning king. The quarters near the hoist are the royal arms, and those in the fly those of her own family, Bowes-Lyon.

Children of the sovereign use the royal arms with labels like that on the standard of Prince Charles, but with distinguishing marks on the points. Princess Margaret (as daughter of George
11 VI) has a thistle and two roses on her points, and Princess Anne

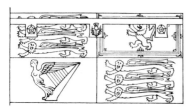

HRH Princess Margaret

a red heart and two red crosses. The Duke of Kent, as the grandson of a previous monarch, has a label of five points, and on these three blue anchors and two red crosses.

Although other members of the royal family, such as the Duke of Gloucester, have their own arms, they normally use a special standard consisting of the royal banner with an ermine border all round. H.R.H. the Princess of Wales has a personal coat of arms and a coat of arms used jointly with the Prince of Wales, but as yet has not adopted a personal flag or standard.

NATIONAL FLAGS

The national flag of the United Kingdom, the **Union Jack**, is a combination of emblems representing England, Scotland, and Ireland.

The red cross on white of St George dates back to the 12 Crusades, and has been recorded in use as the national emblem of England since at least 1277. The badge was adopted as that of the premier order of chivalry, the Order of the Garter, in 1348, and came into use as a flag early in the fifteenth century. It was by no means the earliest English flag, and in early times banners of other saints were also displayed. At the Battle of Hastings a dragon standard of the kind described in the Introduction (p. 9) was used by the English, and later taken over by the Normans. But after 1348 other emblems were pushed into the background, and (despite their Welsh connections) a great deal of prominence was given to the Cross of St George by the Tudors, in whose time it was first carried round the world by Drake.

The saltire cross of Scotland has a mythological origin, but is 13 truly associated with St Andrew, who was adopted as Scotland's patron saint at a much earlier date than was St George in England. Like the flag of England, though, that of Scotland gradually evolved over centuries into its present form and colours. When the thrones were united in 1603 a unified national emblem was proposed for British ships, and on 12 14

29

38 *Gibraltar:*
ensign badge

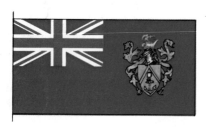

39 *Pitcairn*

40 *New England flag,*
c. 1700

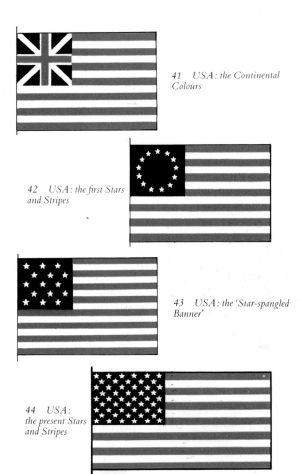

41 USA: the Continental Colours

42 USA: the first Stars and Stripes

43 USA: the 'Star-spangled Banner'

44 USA: the present Stars and Stripes

April 1606 the first Union Jack was adopted. This was to be flown at the main top, and the cross of St George or of St Andrew (according to the country of origin) at the fore top. In 1624, however, the Union Jack was reserved for ships in the royal service, and was never again permitted to merchant ships in its plain form. These then began to use red flags with the national cross in the canton, and this was the origin of the modern Red Ensign. From 1707 onwards merchant ships were permitted to wear the Red Ensign with the whole Union Jack in the canton, a practice confirmed in 1864, although by that date the Union Jack had been altered to its present form. This was introduced on 1 January 1801, following the Act of Union with Ireland. The new design incorporated the red saltire cross attributed to St Patrick, for Ireland, in a counterchanged form so as to combine it with the saltire of St Andrew. The shape and form used today evolved at sea in the nineteenth century, and do not conform exactly to the original specifications.

It is now considered pedantic to refer to the national flag as the 'Union Flag', since 'Union Jack' has become so familiar. With regard to flying it the right way up, it is only necessary to note that the broad white band of the cross of St Andrew should be above the red band of the cross of St Patrick in the upper hoist canton. Scouts use the useful mnemonic 'Broad White Top' to remember this. An interesting exercise for budding vexillologists is to count how many Union Jacks are upside down in displays of pageantry.

Despite its lack of official status the Union Jack is now universally used on land as the British national flag. There are no specifications for its use on land, although the Army has adopted its own. It does not have to have any particular proportions or colour shades, and there is no code of protocol for its use. It may only be used at sea, however, in certain specific circumstances, although it has now become customary to paint it on the fuselages of British aircraft.

In 1864 the present system of **ensigns** for use at sea was

adopted. The Red Ensign was allocated to the merchant service; 16
the White Ensign, formerly one of three naval ensigns, was 17
reserved for the Royal Navy, and the Blue Ensign was assigned 18
to ships in the government service. The Red and Blue Ensigns
could be used, with badges in the fly, by ships of the British
colonies, and are still so used by some today (see, for example
Bermuda, p. 45). Badges of various branches of government
could be added to the Blue Ensign, and with an upright gold
anchor in the fly it is also the ensign for the Royal Fleet
Auxiliaries.

The correct flag for British registered civilian vessels is the
Red Ensign, usually flown at the stern. Certain yacht clubs have
the right to fly differenced Red or Blue Ensigns, and one, the
Royal Yacht Squadron, may fly the White Ensign. Other flags
(club burgees, owner's flags, the flags of shipping lines, etc.) may
be flown in subordinate positions.

DEFENCE FORCES

The defence forces are frequent users of flags. Following the
creation of the unified Ministry of Defence in 1964 a Joint
Services flag was introduced for use at headquarters where all
three branches of the services are working together. This is in
the blue, red and light blue colours of the three services, with
the 'tri-service' badge in the centre. There is also a distinguishing
flag for the Chief of the Defence Staff, who is the principal 19
'unified' commander of the defence forces. This is in the same
colours, arranged horizontally, with the Union Jack in the
canton and the tri-service badge in the fly. The badge is encircled
by the Garter, dating from the appointment of Lord Louis
Mountbatten as Chief of Defence Staff in 1965. Other members
of the Joint Staff have similar flags which may be flown from
their cars or headquarters.

The flag of the **Navy** is the White Ensign (see above). The
Union Jack is used as a jack only by vessels of the Royal Navy. 17

45   *USA: President*

46   *USA: Vice-President*

47   *USA: ceremonial flag of Army*

48   USA: *ceremonial flag of Navy*

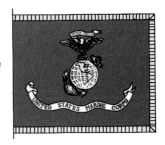

49   USA: *ceremonial flag of Marine Corps*

50   USA: *ceremonial flag of Air Force*

Rank flags are used in the Navy and the Royal Air Force. The
20 highest rank in the Navy is the Lord High Admiral, an office
now an honorary title of the sovereign. By virtue of it she is
entitled to a flag which dates back to the early seventeenth
century. An Admiral of the Fleet is entitled to fly the Union
Jack, a practice also dating back to the seventeenth century. An
Admiral flies the plain cross of St George, the ancient flag of
England. A Vice-Admiral adds a red disc to the canton, and a
Rear-Admiral another in the lower hoist. A Commodore has a
broad pendant of St George with a red disc in the canton. A
Commodore on the active list of the Royal Naval Reserve has
a broad white pendant with a blue cross. The Commandant-
General of the Royal Marines has a blue rank flag with a badge
of an anchor and the royal crest, all in yellow. Other officers of
the Royal Marines have similar flags. The Sea Cadet Corps uses
the Blue Ensign with its badge in the fly.

21   The **Army** ensign for use on land was introduced in 1938,
and has the Army badge in yellow on a red field. Rank flags are
not officially assigned to the Army, although many appoint-
ments carry distinguishing flags, such as the Chief of the General
Staff who flies the Union Jack with the Royal Crest in the
centre. The flag of a senior commander in the field is the plain
Union Jack. There is also an Army ensign for use on vessels in
the Army's service, and there are distinctive additions to the
Union Jack for commanding officers afloat.

22   The **RAF** ensign was introduced in 1920 and is used at all
RAF establishments. In the centre of the fly is the RAF roundel
adopted during the First World War, which is painted on all
RAF planes. A Marshal of the RAF has a distinguishing flag
23 dating from about 1917, with a pattern of red, light blue, and
dark blue stripes. The eight senior ranks of the RAF are entitled
to similar distinguishing flags, the use of which was regulated
in 1938. Since 1942 the Commandant of the RAF Regiment
has been permitted to use the flag of an Air-Vice-Marshal (like
that of a Marshal but with only one horizontal red stripe) with

the regimental badge superimposed. As in the Army there are also flags for the senior commanders, e.g. the Director of the WRAF has a light blue flag with the roundel in the centre, on which is superimposed the 'astral' crown of the RAF.

There are two subsidiary organizations attached to the RAF which have special flags. The Royal Observer Corps uses the RAF Ensign, but with its badge in place of the roundel, as does the Air Training Corps. Ocean Weather Ships come under the control of the Air Force Board, but they too use the naval Blue Ensign with their badge in the fly.

GOVERNMENT
AND NATIONAL CORPORATIONS

A very large number of government departments, national boards and corporations, and statutory bodies have adopted flags both for sea and land use. Many departments directly under government control use the Blue Ensign with a distinctive badge. Among these should be mentioned the Customs and Excise and the Coast Guard. The ensign of the Customs service bears the ancient badge of a portcullis that has been in use since the seventeenth century. The Coast Guard badge is a new one, 24 granted on 28 October 1974; before this the service had no flag.

Among the public corporations which can be mentioned is British Airways, the national airline, which has a flag based on 25 its coat of arms. All airports and civil air establishments are entitled to use the civil air ensign and this may also be used on 26 the ground by British aircraft. Aircraft carrying the royal mail are entitled to a blue pennant with the royal crown, and bugle, and the legend *Royal Mail*, all in yellow. This is often painted on the fuselage. Other public corporations with distinctive flags are: British Rail, whose distinctive red flag dates from 1966; 27 the National Bus Company which has a white flag charged with its 'logo' in blue and red; and the British Broadcasting Corporation, which uses a banner of its arms, which contain the globe seen revolving on television screens.

51   USA: ceremonial
flag of Coast Guard

52   'Flag of the South'
(the Confederate States)

53   Alabama

54   Alaska

55 *Arizona*

56 *Arkansas*

57 *California*

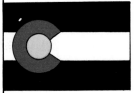

58 *Colorado*

The above are only a few of the very many flags in common use, but there are also many regional and civic flags, and a wide variety of public and private organizations making use of flags today.

COUNTRIES OF THE UNITED KINGDOM

Most parts of the United Kingdom have flags for local use, although unless otherwise stated these are not for use at sea, and do not have the status of national flags.

12 **England**   The flag of England is the cross of St George, red on a white field. It is traditionally flown on 23 April.

13 **Scotland**   The flag of Scotland is the saltire of St Andrew, white on blue, although much use is made of the Red Lion flag, the royal banner of Scotland. Because it is a royal flag the heraldic authorities try to restrain its use by the public—not always successfully, despite a law of 1558 which makes its illegal use punishable by death!

28 **Wales**   The flag of Wales is known as the Red Dragon, *Y Ddraig Goch*, and it is now widely used, following its offical approval in 1959.

29 **Northern Ireland**   A flag for local use was approved in 1953. It is a banner of the arms granted to the Government of Northern Ireland, which display the Red Hand of the O'Neills on a star of six points, representing the 'Six Counties' of Northern Ireland.

30 **Isle of Man**   The flag of the Isle of Man is of ancient origin, and bears the Three Legs of Man emblem which is also the coat of arms. There is also a civil ensign: the Red Ensign with the Three Legs emblem (also known as the *Trinacria*) in the fly.

Jersey   The flag of Jersey is said to date back to the fifteenth century. It is white with a red saltire, similar to that attributed to St Patrick, together with a crowned shield of arms, added in 1981. The arms are the same as those of England. The Lieutenant-Governor uses the Union Jack with the shield within a laurel garland in the centre.

Guernsey   Guernsey adopted new flags for use on land and at sea in 1985. The flag for use on land is the Cross of St George, as used previously, but with the addition of a golden inner cross, representing Duke William of Normandy, who had such a cross on the flag he used at the Battle of Hastings. In the flag for use at sea, which is the usual British Red Ensign, this cross is used as a badge in the fly. This makes Guernsey the only one of the Channel Islands to have a distinctive flag for use at sea. Three of Guernsey's dependencies also have flags:

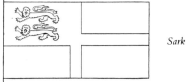

Sark

Sark   The flag is a combination of the arms of Normandy with the flag of England.

.Alderney   The flag is like that of England, with a circular badge of green with a gold lion, placed in the centre of the cross.

Herm   A flag was adopted in 1984, also based on the cross of St George. In this case the Arms of Herm, showing three cowled

59 *Connecticut*

60 *Delaware*

61 *Florida*

62 *Georgia*

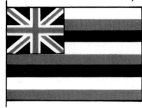

63 *Hawaii*

64 Idaho

65 Illinois

66 Indiana

67 Iowa

68 Kansas

monks on a golden diagonal stripe between blue triangles charged with silver dolphins, appear in rectangular form in the canton.

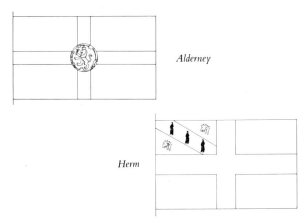

Alderney

Herm

DEPENDENCIES
OF THE UNITED KINGDOM

In the following section the date given after each name is the date the territory was permanently acquired by Britain. It is to be noted that those dependencies with more distinctive flags are in looser relationship with Britain than those which merely use ensign badges in the fly of the Blue Ensign. The Governors of colonies and Associated States are entitled to use their badge or arms in the centre of the Union Jack, on a white disc surrounded by a wreath of laurel.

Anguilla (1650) Formerly a part of St Christopher-Nevis, Anguilla broke away in May 1967. Its position was regularized as a direct dependency of the UK in February 1976. The flag was adopted in October 1967, and was designed by a New York artist.

Bermuda (1609)   This is one of Britain's oldest colonies, and has a shield dating from soon after its establishment, but regularized in 1910. The shield portrays the wreck of the *Sea Venture* in 1609 when Sir George Somers and his settlers first reached Bermuda. In 1915 it was added to the fly of the Red Ensign without any background, and this is now the flag for general use.

British Antarctic Territory (1962)   Formerly part of the Falkland Islands Dependencies this Territory was formed in March 1962. Ships engaged in research work there fly the Blue Ensign with the shield only from the arms, in the fly. The arms are an embellished form of those granted to the Falkland Islands Dependency in 1952. The shield symbolizes research in waters and regions of ice.

British Antarctic
Territory: arms

British Virgin Islands (1672)   The arms of the Virgin Islands date from 1909, regularized in November 1960. The shield bears a virgin, as in the gospel story, and twelve lamps. The shield alone appears on the fly of the Blue Ensign.

Cayman Islands (1665)   Formerly a dependency of Jamaica

69   Kentucky

70   Louisiana

71   Maine

72   Maryland

73   Massachusetts

74   *Michigan*

75   *Minnesota*

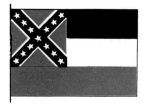

76   *Mississippi*

77   *Missouri*

British Virgin Islands: ensign badge

36 the Cayman Islands became a separate colony in August 1962. A coat of arms was granted in May 1958, and this appears on a white disc in the fly of the Blue Ensign. The stars stand for the three main islands.

Falkland Islands (1833)   These islands were first discovered
37 by an Englishman, John Davis, in 1592. His ship, the *Desire*, is portrayed in the coat of arms granted in September 1948, and referred to in the motto. The arms appear on a white disc in the Blue Ensign. The flag of the Governor, now used by the Civil Administrator, is the Union Jack with the Arms of the Falkland Islands on a white disc within a garland of laurel leaves placed in the centre.

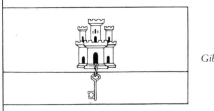

Gibraltar

Gibraltar (1713)   Gibraltar has a coat of arms granted by Ferdinand and Isabella in 1502. The arms appear in the fly of
38 the Blue Ensign to form the flag for use at sea, and in circular form in the centre of the Union Jack, within a laurel garland, to form the Governor's flag. On the Blue Ensign the arms include the scroll with the motto *Montis Insignia Calpe* ('The

sign of Mount Calpe') and are set on a white disc. There is also a flag for the City, which is a banner of the arms. The use of the arms as a basis for the flags was regularized in 1982.

Hong Kong: ensign badge

Hong Kong (1841)   The coat of arms was granted in January 1959, and appears on a white disc on the Blue Ensign. The colony lies at the mouth of the Pearl River, whose name is referred to by the pearl held by the lion in the crest. A competition is under way to find a distinctive local flag for Hong Kong when it becomes a Special Region of China in 1997.

Montserrat (1763)   Montserrat became a separate colony in 1962, but has a shield which dates back to at least 1909 when it was part of the Leeward Islands colony. The shield now appears on a white disc on the Blue Ensign.

Montserrat: ensign badge

78 *Montana*

79 *Nebraska*

80 *Nevada*

81 *New Hampshire*

82 *New Jersey*

83　New Mexico

84　New York

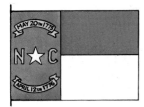

85　North Carolina

86　North Dakota

Pitcairn (1887)   A flag for Pitcairn was introduced in 1984, and shows the whole Arms, as granted in 1969, in the fly of a British Blue Ensign. This is for use on land and at sea.

St Helena (1659)   St Helena was acquired by the East India Company in 1659 and became a crown colony in 1854. For many years it used a locally-designed badge on the Blue Ensign, but on 30 January 1984 it was granted a complete coat of arms. The shield from this now appears on the Blue Ensign. Over the scene of an East Indiaman is a yellow chief with a wirebird in natural colours. This ensign is also used by **Ascension Island** and **Tristan da Cunha**.

Turks and Caicos Islands (1672)   These islands were formerly a dependency of Jamaica and became a separate colony in 1962, although linked to the Bahamas until April 1973. A separate coat of arms was granted in September 1965, and the shield from this was placed on the fly of the Blue Ensign in November 1968. It bears a shell, a lobster, and a cactus.

St Helena: ensign badge

Turks and Caicos Islands: arms

THE UNITED STATES OF AMERICA

THE STARS AND STRIPES

The Stars and Stripes, the national flag of the United States, has evolved over a long period since the outbreak of the War of Independence in April 1775. Before this time a flag of nine alternating red and white stripes had been used by a protest movement called the 'Sons of Liberty': the nine stripes standing for the colonies in revolt against the Stamp Act. At Bunker Hill in June 1775 a red flag with a pine tree (also a symbol of liberty) on a white canton was used on the American side, and a pine tree flag was also used on rebel ships later that year. These seem to have developed from a flag used in New England in the early 40 eighteenth century. In December 1775 when Washington mustered the Continental Army at Cambridge, Massachusetts, a flag known as the 'Continental Colours' was hoisted. This was 41 a flag of thirteen red and white stripes, with the British Union Jack in the canton. The thirteen stripes stood for the colonies, and the canton (or 'Union') for the British connection. This was misconstrued, however, as a sign of submission, and so a new canton was eventually inserted, by resolution of the Continental Congress, in June 1777. A canton of stars may have been 42 derived from the flag of Rhode Island, or from already-established military colours, but it is probable that it was the first alternative to suggest itself. Some writers assert that the stars were placed in a pattern like the cross and saltire in the Union Jack, which would reinforce this view.

The Stars and Stripes was intended to have a star and a stripe for each colony. It is now a common belief that the stars were arranged in a circle and that Betsy Ross persuaded the Congress to use a five-pointed star when she made the first flag, but there is no evidence for any of this. In 1795 the number of stars and

53

87   Ohio

88   Oklahoma

89   Oregon

90   Pennsylvania

91   Rhode Island

92   South Carolina

93   South Dakota

94   Tennessee

95   Texas

43 stripes was increased to fifteen, producing a flag known as the 'Star-spangled Banner', as in the American national anthem. But in 1818 the stripes were put back to thirteen, and from then on new states were represented by new stars only, to be added on the 4 July following their admission. The last alteration, to fifty stars, was made on 4 July 1960, following the admission of Hawaii.

44 The national flag is also the civil and naval ensign. The jack is the canton from the national flag.

FLAGS OF THE GOVERNMENT
45 The flag of the President is blue with the arms within a ring of fifty stars, a pattern introduced in 1945. The flag of the Vice-
46 President is based on this but was altered in 1975. It is white with the full arms in the centre, and four blue stars in the cantons. The four stars denote a member of the Cabinet and are also used on the distinguishing flags of other members of the Government.

DEFENCE FORCES
The Secretary of Defence has a flag of blue with four white stars in the cantons, and in the centre a stylized eagle grasping three arrows (for the three services). The flag of the Secretary of the

USA: Secretary of Defence

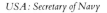
USA: Secretary of Navy   USA: Secretary of Army

Navy is similar, with four stars, and a large foul anchor, all in white. This dates back to 1866. The flag of the Secretary of the Army is red, also with four stars, and the whole national arms in full colour in the centre. This dates from 1897. The flag of the Secretary of the Air Force is in the intermediate blue used by that service, with the four stars, and the Air Force coat of arms in the centre. Rank flags for all three services are the same, except for the field colour, which is red for the Army, dark blue for the Navy, and intermediate blue for the Air Force. They all have the same pattern of large white stars, i.e. five for a Fleet Admiral and a General of the Army or of the Air Force, four for an Admiral and a General and so on, the number of stars decreasing for the lower ranks. A maroon field is used by

USA: Secretary
of the Air Force

96   Utah

97   Vermont

98   Virginia

99   Washington

100   *West Virginia*

101   *Wisconsin*

102   *Wyoming*

103   *District of Columbia*

Generals of the Army Medical Service, and a purple one by the Chaplain's Department. Admirals not in command at sea have their stars in blue on white.

Each branch of the Services has a ceremonial standard, although copies of them are issued in quantity. The Army flag dates from June 1956, although its central emblem dates back to 1777. The date on the flag, *1775,* is the date the Continental Army was raised. The Navy flag dates from April 1959, although the central seal goes back to 1798. The Marine Corps flag dates from 1939, with the well-known badge, not unlike that of the British Royal Marines, in the centre. The eagle bears a ribbon with the motto *Semper Fidelis* ('Always Faithful'). The Air Force flag has the same blue as that used for rank flags, with the Air Force emblem in the centre within a ring of thirteen stars. The Coast Guard also has a ceremonial flag, bearing the US arms in the centre and the name above, with the motto *Semper Paratus* ('Always Ready') and the date, *1790,* when the Coast Guard was founded. There is a special flag for Coast Guard ships, dating from August 1799, with sixteen vertical stripes (this was before it was decided to reduce the number of stripes on the national flag to thirteen), the arms on a white canton, and the badge in the fly. The flag of the Customs Service is like this, but without the badge. The USA also has a special

USA: Coast Guard ensign

Ensign for Yachts, for specially registered vessels, which is like the national flag but with a foul anchor within a ring of thirteen stars in the canton in place of the fifty stars. This dates from 1848. The Power Squadron ensign is similar, but with blue vertical stripes, and the emblem in white on a red canton.

FLAGS OF THE CONFEDERATE STATES

The 'Flag of the South' is a flag still widely used in those states 52 which were once part of the Confederate States of America, 1861–5. The flag is that adopted as the jack of the Confederate navy in 1863, but it came to be widely regarded as the actual national flag. In square form, with a white border, it was the battle flag of the southern states. The thirteen stars represent the adherents of the Confederacy, not the original thirteen states of the Union. It will be noted that several states which were once part of the Confederacy have flags which are based on the Flag of the South, or on the Stars and Bars, the first true national flag of the South. For this reason the former members are marked (CSA) in the list on pp. 64–5.

FLAGS OF THE STATES

Each state of the Union has its own arms (or seal) and flag. In the following list the date is given of the state's admission to the Union or, in the case of the original thirteen, of its ratification of the Constitution. The second date is that of the adoption of the present design of the state flag. It should be noted, however, that many states had previous designs. The flags of California, Hawaii, and Texas were those of independent nations before they joined the USA.

Many state flags are simply blue fields with the arms or seal in the centre. These often derive from military colours carried in the nineteenth century, or were inspired by the first Centennial in 1876. Some of the flags of red, white, and blue

104   Guam

105   Micronesia:
national flag

106   Puerto Rico

107   Virgin Islands
of the USA

*108 Afghanistan:
national flag*

*109 Albania:
national flag*

*110 Algeria:
national flag*

*111 Andorra:
national flag*

refer not to the Confederacy or the Union but to the French territory of Louisiana, from which several of the states were carved. Flags with red and yellow usually refer to the rule of Spain.

	State	Date of Admission	Present Flag Adopted
53	Alabama (CSA)	14 December 1819	16 February 1895
54	Alaska	3 January 1959	2 May 1927
55	Arizona	14 February 1912	27 February 1927
56	Arkansas (CSA)	15 June 1836	4 April 1924
57	California	9 December 1850	3 February 1911
58	Colorado	1 August 1876	5 June 1911
59	Connecticut	9 January 1788	4 July 1895
60	Delaware	7 December 1787	24 July 1913
61	Florida (CSA)	3 March 1845	6 November 1900
62	Georgia (CSA)	2 January 1788	1 July 1956
63	Hawaii	18 March 1959	20 May 1845
64	Idaho	3 July 1890	12 March 1907
65	Illinois	3 December 1818	1 July 1970
66	Indiana	11 December 1816	31 March 1921
67	Iowa	28 December 1846	29 March 1921
68	Kansas	29 January 1861	30 June 1963
69	Kentucky	1 June 1792	26 March 1918
70	Louisiana (CSA)	30 April 1812	1 July 1912
71	Maine	15 March 1820	24 February 1909
72	Maryland	28 April 1788	9 March 1904
73	Massachusetts	6 February 1788	6 March 1915
74	Michigan	26 March 1837	1 August 1911
75	Minnesota	11 May 1858	19 March 1957
76	Mississippi (CSA)	10 December 1817	7 February 1894
77	Missouri	10 August 1821	22 March 1913
78	Montana	8 November 1889	27 February 1905
79	Nebraska	1 March 1867	2 April 1925
80	Nevada	31 October 1864	26 March 1929
81	New Hampshire	21 June 1787	26 March 1896
82	New Jersey	18 December 1787	26 March 1896
83	New Mexico	6 January 1912	15 March 1925
84	New York	26 July 1787	2 April 1901
85	North Carolina (CSA)	21 November 1789	9 March 1885
86	North Dakota	2 November 1889	3 March 1911
87	Ohio	1 March 1803	9 May 1902

State	Date of Admission	Present Flag Adopted	
Oklahoma	16 November 1907	9 May 1941	88
Oregon	14 February 1859	26 February 1925	89
Pennsylvania	12 December 1787	13 June 1907	90
Rhode Island	29 May 1790	19 May 1897	91
South Carolina (CSA)	23 May 1788	28 January 1861	92
South Dakota	2 November 1889	11 March 1963	93
Tennessee (CSA)	7 June 1796	17 April 1905	94
Texas (CSA)	29 December 1845	25 January 1839	95
Utah	4 January 1896	11 March 1913	96
Vermont	4 March 1791	1 June 1923	97
Virginia (CSA)	25 June 1788	30 April 1861	98
Washington	11 November 1889	7 June 1923	99
West Virginia	20 June 1863	7 March 1929	100
Wisconsin	29 May 1848	29 April 1913	101
Wyoming	10 July 1890	31 January 1917	102

District of Columbia This is not a state but a Federal District. It contains the capital, Washington, and it is not surprising that the flag is the banner of arms of George 103 Washington. This was adopted in 1938. The arms are those of the Washington family from Sulgrave Manor, Northamptonshire, England.

DEPENDENCIES OF THE USA

American Samoa The flag was adopted in April 1960. The eagle is for the USA, and it is grasping a staff, called a *fue*, and a

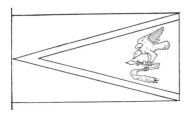

American Samoa

112 Angola:
national flag

113 Antigua-Barbuda

114 Argentina:
national flag
and naval ensign

115 Australia:
national flag
and jack

116 Australia:
Queen's personal flag

117 Western Australia

118 New South Wales

119 Queensland

120 Tasmania

121 Victoria

122 South Australia

club, *uatogi*, Samoan symbols of sovereignty. The field of the flag is dark blue, with a white triangle, fimbriated (bordered in) red. The eagle is in natural colours, and the *fue* and *uatogi* are yellow. The eastern part of Samoa was taken over by the USA in 1900.

Federated States of Micronesia Micronesia now consists of the states of Kosrae, Ponape, Truk, and Yap, each with flags of their own. These four states form a federation under US Trusteeship. Palau, the North Marianas, and the Marshall Islands, formerly part of the Trust Territory, are now separate autonomous units. The federal flag was adopted in November 1978, and is based on the original one adopted on United Nations Day 1962. The field represents the UN and the four 105 stars the states. **Palau.** The flag is blue with a yellow disc, and was adopted on 13 June 1980. **Marshall Islands.** The flag was adopted on 1 May 1979, and has a dark blue field with two rays, orange over white, and a white sun of 24 rays in the hoist. **North Marianas.** The flag is UN blue with a grey *latte* stone on a white star.

Guam Guam was acquired by the USA from Spain in 1898. 104 The flag was adopted in July 1917.

Puerto Rico Originally Spanish, Puerto Rico was acquired 106 in 1899. Its flag dates from the revolutionary movement of 1895. It was made official in July 1952. The design is based on that of Cuba.

Palau

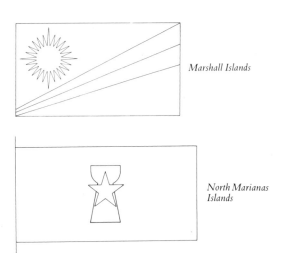

Marshall Islands

North Marianas Islands

Virgin Islands of the United States These islands were bought from Denmark in March 1917. A local flag was adopted in May 1921, based on the arms of the USA. 107

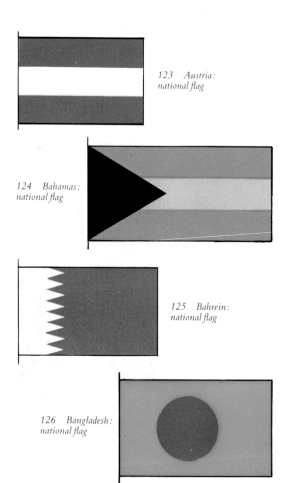

123   Austria:
national flag

124   Bahamas:
national flag

125   Bahrein:
national flag

126   Bangladesh:
national flag

70

127　Barbados: national
flag and civil ensign

128a　Belgium:
civil ensign

128b　Belgium:
royal standard

129　Belize:
national flag

130　Benin:
national flag

A TO Z OF NATIONS

108 **Afghanistan** The flag of Afghanistan was revised on 21 April 1980, following a change of regime. It reverts to the old colours of black, red, and green placed horizontally, rather like the flag of 1974–78. The emblem in the hoist contains several traditional elements: the pulpit of a mosque, a holy book, a rising sun, and a wreath of wheat-ears. The ribbon in the national colours is now without any inscription.

109 **Albania** The national flag was adopted in 1912, but uses an emblem dating back to the Byzantine Empire. The red star was added in 1946, following the formation of the People's Republic. The Albanians call their country *Shqipëria*, the Land of the Eagle.

110 **Algeria** The flag of Algeria was officially adopted when the country became independent in 1962, although it had been used by the liberation movement for some years prior to this.

111 **Andorra** The flag in its present form dates from 1866. The arms do not always appear in the centre, and their quarterings vary somewhat. However, they always represent: Urgel (the mitre and crozier), Foix (three red stripes on yellow), Catalonia (four red stripes on yellow), and Béarn (the two cows). The motto is *Virtus Unita Fortior* ('United Strength is Greater').

112 **Angola** The flag of Angola was adopted when independence was declared in November 1975, and is based on that of the dominant liberation movement, the MPLA.

113 **Antigua-Barbuda** The former Associated State of Antigua became independent under this name on 1 November 1981, but retained the flag and arms adopted in 1967. The flag was

72

designed by a local art teacher and was the winning entry in a competition. The rising sun on a black field over a blue and white sea represents the dawn of a new era for the inhabitants, whose dynamism is expressed by the red background.

Argentina The flag of Argentina has colours dating from 114 1810, when independence from Spain was declared. The 'Sun of May' became the symbol of emancipation, and was added to the flag in 1818. The flag for general use does not have the sun. The blue is derived from the blue skies on the day independence was declared, and the sun from its appearance on that day.

Australia The Australian flag was adopted in 1901, shortly 115 after independence was achieved. The design consists of three parts: the Union Jack representing the British connection, the stars of the Southern Cross for Australia itself, and the 'Commonwealth Star', which has seven points, one for each state and one for the dependent territories.

Queen Elizabeth II has a special flag for use in Australia, 116 consisting of a banner of the arms, with the same device as in her other personal standards (see p. 25) in the centre, superimposed on a large golden version of the Commonwealth Star. The civil ensign is the same as the national flag, but with a red field. The naval ensign is also similar, with a white field and the stars in blue. The Governor-General, like those of other Commonwealth countries which are not republics, has a flag of royal blue, with the royal crest in the centre, and beneath this a gold scroll with the name of the country in black letters: in this case, *Commonwealth of Australia*.

Each state has a distinctive form of the Blue Ensign, with its badge in the fly, dating from the time when they were separate colonies. These badges are derived from, or form part of, their coats of arms. The oldest is that of **Western Australia**, dating 117 from 1875 and portraying a black swan. Those of **New South** 118 **Wales**, **Queensland**, and **Tasmania** were adopted in 1876 119 120

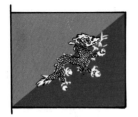

131 Bhutan:
national flag

132 Bolivia: national
flag and civil ensign

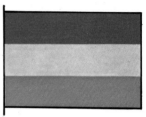

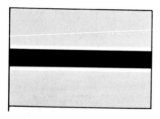

133 Botswana:
national flag

134 Brazil: national
flag and civil ensign

135 Brunei

136 *Bulgaria:*
national flag

137 *Burkina*
Faso

138 *Burma:*
national flag

139 *Burundi:*
national flag

140 *Cameroun:*
national flag

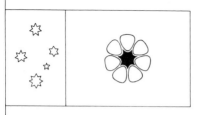

Australia:
Northern
Territory

and are based on parts of their coats of arms. The badge of
121 **Victoria** dates from 1877, but may be older in origin. That of
122 **South Australia** was not adopted until 1904.

The **Northern Territory** has a very distinctive flag which
was adopted on 1 July 1978. The hoist is black, with stars like
those of the national flag, and the fly is ochre, with a
representation of the desert rose in black and white. There is
also a flag for **Norfolk Island**, adopted in 1980. It has three
vertical strips of green, white, green, with a green pine tree in
the centre. None of the other dependent territories have
distinctive flags.

Norfolk Island

Austria   The Austrian flag is one of the oldest in continuous   123
use. The red and white stripes are from the arms of the early
dukes, dating back to at least 1230, and possibly to the time of
Leopold V, who was supposed to have had his white surcoat
drenched in blood, except for the part under his sword-belt.
The national flag is plain, but the State flag and ensign has the
arms over all in the centre. The arms are a black spread eagle
with the shield on its breast. In its claws are a hammer and
sickle, added in 1921, and on its legs broken chains, symbolizing
the liberation of the country in 1945.

Each of the nine states has its own arms and flag.

Bahamas   The colours of the flag of the Bahamas, adopted in   124
July 1973, represent the blue seas and golden sands of the islands
and the strength of their people. The official specifications
require that the blue is of the same aquamarine as the seas
around the islands.

Bahrein   Bahrein is one of many states in the Persian Gulf
with a red and white flag. The serrated white strip was added   125
to make it more distinctive. There is also a flag for the ruler,
which adds white borders to the top and bottom edges of the
national flag.

Bangladesh   The first flag of Bangladesh had a gold map of
the country on the red disc, but this was removed in 1972. The   126
green field signifies the fertile land, and the red disc the struggle
for freedom. The civil ensign is red with the national flag in the
canton. The red disc is not in the exact centre of the flag, but set
slightly towards the hoist.

Barbados   The flag of Barbados was adopted when the island   127
became independent in 1966. The colours represent the blue
seas and the golden sands, and the trident is derived from the
former colonial badge. There is a flag for the Governor-General
of the same pattern as that for Australia (see p. 73), which is the
usual pattern, and also a flag for the Prime Minister.

*141 Canada:
national flag
and civil and
naval ensign*

*142 Canada:
Queen's personal flag*

143 Alberta

144 British Columbia

145   Manitoba

146   New Brunswick

147   Newfoundland

148   Nova Scotia

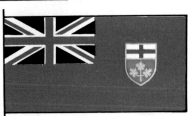

49   Ontario

Belgium   The Belgian colours first appeared in the Belgian revolt against the Austrians in 1789, and were used again in 1830 when the Belgians campaigned for freedom from the Dutch. The colours are said to derive from the arms of Brabant, a gold lion with red tongue and claws on a black shield, now used as the national arms. The national flag differs from the civil ensign in that the former is almost square and the latter 2:3.

128
a

128   The royal standard is in a dark shade of red with the crowned
b   shield in the centre, and the royal cypher in each corner. The Queen and male members of the royal family have similar flags with their respective initials.

The naval and military ensign is of modern design but uses the saltire, found on local flags since the Middle Ages (Belgium was once part of Burgundy, whose flag was a red 'saltire raguly' on white). The Air Force ensign has the badge of the Air Force in the canton, and the Air Force roundel in the centre.

Flags representing the Walloon and Flemish communities are now widely used in Belgium. The Walloon flag has a red cockerel on a yellow field and the Flemish one a black lion rampant on a yellow field.

Belize   Belize became independent on 21 September 1981 and adopted a flag based on the previous unofficial flag for use
129 on land. This was blue with a white disc containing the arms within a laurel garland. The new flag adds a red stripe to the top and bottom, and also uses a slightly revised form of the arms.

Benin   This is the country known as Dahomey until November 1975. The original flag was yellow over red with a green strip in the hoist—a colour combination known as the Pan-African colours—but since becoming the People's Republic
130 of Benin the flag has been plain green, to emphasize the

agricultural economy, with a red star in the canton, standing
for the revolution and for national unity.

Bhutan   Bhutan has a flag with the same sort of dragon as   131
used to appear on the flags of China. The layout of the flag has
changed several times in recent years, but the present design
was adopted when Bhutan was admitted to the United Nations.
The name of the country in its own language is *Druk Yul*, the
Land of the Dragon.

Bolivia   The national flag achieved its present form in   132
November 1851, although it employs colours used on earlier
flags since 1825. The national flag is the plain tricolour, whose
colours are taken to represent valour, and the mineral and
agricultural wealth of the country. The State flag and President's
flag have the national arms in the centre, the main feature of
which is the silver mountain of Potosí: the nine stars stand for
the provinces.

150   *Prince Edward Island*

151   *Quebec*

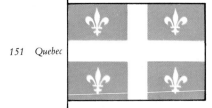

152
Saskatchewan

153   *North-West Territories*

154   Yukon

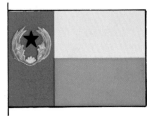

*155   Cape Verde Islands:
national flag*

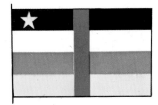

*156   Central Africa:
national flag*

*157   Chad:
national flag*

83

133 **Botswana**   The colours of the flag of Botswana, adopted on achieving independence in September 1966, stand for rain, and for the black and white population. The word for rain is *Pula*, and this is the motto on the coat of arms, which, on a white disc with a black border on a light blue flag, constitutes the President's standard.

134 **Brazil**   Many features of the flag of Brazil are derived from those of Portugal, which ruled there until 1822. From then until 1889 Brazil was an independent empire, but when the republic was established the royal arms in the centre of the flag were changed to a celestial sphere. This has twenty-two stars, representing the states, scattered over its surface. They are arranged in the pattern seen in the night sky over Rio de Janeiro. The motto around the equator reads *Ordem E Progresso* ('Order and Progress'). The national flag is also the civil and naval ensign. The jack is dark blue with a cross made of twenty-two stars.

The President's standard is green with the whole arms in the centre. These feature the constellation of the Southern Cross, as in the flag of Australia, within a border of twenty-two stars.

Each federal state has its own arms and flag, some of considerable antiquity. The Federal District, and the capital, Brasilia, each have their own flag, the constitution of Brazil being rather similar to that of the USA. Several of the state flags employ the Southern Cross to symbolize their location in the southern hemisphere.

135 **Brunei**   Brunei became fully independent on 1 January 1985 but retained all its flags and emblems. The national flag dates from 1906. The yellow field represents the Sultan, the white stripe the people, and the black one the government. Over-all in the centre are the Arms of the state in red. On the crescent is a motto which means 'Always render service with God's guidance', and on the scroll 'Brunei, Abode of Peace'. The arms were added to the flag in 1959.

Bulgaria   The colours date from 1878, when the country achieved independence. The national emblem was placed in the canton in 1947, but it has been modified since then. The present emblem retains the ancient lion rampant, but has it treading on a cogwheel. On the scroll are the dates 681, representing the establishment of the first Bulgar state, and 1944, for the liberation from fascism. This is also the civil ensign. The naval ensign is white with narrow stripes of green and red along the bottom edge and a large red star near the hoist. The jack is red with a large white-bordered red star in the centre.

Burkina Faso   The Republic of Upper Volta became Burkina Faso on 4 August 1984 and adopted a new national flag. This is red over green with a yellow star in the centre, thus employing the pan-African colours used by many of its neighbours.

Burma   The canton of the flag of Burma was altered in January 1974 from the design adopted on achieving independence in 1948. The present design signifies the union of agriculture and industry, and has a ring of fourteen stars, for the constituent states.

Burma previously had a range of other flags, including a civil ensign of blue over red with the emblem in the canton, and a naval ensign of white with a red cross throughout and the emblem in white on a blue canton, but it is not certain that these are still in use.

Burundi   The three stars in the centre of the flag of Burundi symbolize the national motto: Unity, Work, Progress. The flag was originally adopted when Burundi became independent as a kingdom in 1962, but it had a drum and a sorghum plant in the centre. After the republic was established in 1966, these emblems were replaced by the three stars.

Cameroun   This country was formerly divided into mandated territories under Britain and France. The French part became independent in 1960 with a plain tricolour in the Pan-

*158   Chile: national flag
and civil ensign*

*159   China:
national flag*

160   Taiwan: national flag

*161   Colombia:
national flag
and civil ensign*

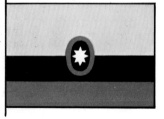

162   Comoro Islands:
national flag

163   Congo:
national flag

164   Costa Rica:
national flag
and civil ensign

165   Cuba: national flag
and civil and naval ensign

87

African colours. When the British part joined it in 1961 two gold stars were placed in the canton. In 1975, to symbolize the unity of the country, these were replaced by a single star in the 140 centre.

Canada Canada existed for a long time without a proper national flag. From 1892 the Red Ensign was in use, with the old arms of Canada in the fly, replaced by the new shield in 1921. From then until 1965 this acted as the *de facto* flag, but it was not universally popular, especially among the French-speaking population. Several attempts were made to design a national flag which would suit everybody, but it was not until 141 February 1965 that an acceptable design was adopted. This is based on the popular red maple leaf emblem, and is now the national flag and civil and naval ensign. The jack is a white flag with the national flag in the canton and the naval emblem in the 142 fly in blue. The Queen's flag for Canada is a banner of the arms, with her cypher in the centre on a blue disc within a chaplet of golden roses. The quarters of the arms represent England, Scotland, France, and Ireland, the countries from which most settlers came; in the base is a red maple leaf for Canada itself. The flag of the Governor-General has the crest from the coat of arms on a royal blue field.

Each province and territory of Canada has its own arms and 143 flag. The flag of **Alberta** has its arms on a blue field, and was 144 adopted in 1968. The flag of **British Columbia**, dating from 145 1960, is a banner of the arms. The flag of **Manitoba** is essentially the British Red Ensign with the shield of the province in the 146 fly; this dates from 1966. The flag of **New Brunswick** is also a banner of its arms, and dates from 1965. The new flag of 147 **Newfoundland** was introduced in 1980 and was designed by a local artist. There is also an unofficial flag of vertical strips of 148 pink, white, green. **Nova Scotia** uses a banner of its arms, 149 which are among the oldest in North America. **Ontario** also uses the Red Ensign, with its shield in the fly. This dates from

1965. **Prince Edward Island** has a banner of its arms, but with a border of the Canadian colours. This was adopted in 1964. **Quebec** has a flag, officially adopted in 1948, known as the *fleurdelysé* flag, which is used throughout the country as a symbol of French separatism. **Saskatchewan** has a flag adopted in 1969 with the shield of arms in the hoist and a prairie lily flower in the fly. The flag of the **North-West Territories** is based on the national flag, in shape although not in colours, and has the shield of arms in the centre. The flag of the **Yukon** is not exactly the same as the national flag in shape, and has the whole arms in the centre. This was adopted in 1968.

150
151
152
153
154

Cape Verde Islands   The Cape Verde Islands, formerly a Portuguese colony, became independent in July 1975, and adopted a flag based on that of the liberation movement. This is in the Pan-African colours, and bears a simplified form of the arms in the red strip. These include a black star and a clamshell. The emblem is set slightly above the centre line.

155

Central Africa   The flag of this country dates back to 1958 and is a combination of the Pan-African colours and those of France. The gold star represents the hope of African unity. During the period 4 December 1976 to 21 December 1979 the country was an 'Empire' under Jean Bokassa. He had a personal standard of green with a golden eagle, but no change was made to the national emblems, which remain the same as when the country became independent in 1960.

156

Chad   The flag of Chad, adopted in 1959, is very similar to that of Andorra, with which it is sometimes confused. The colours are intended to be a compromise between those of France and the African Liberation colours of red, yellow, and green.

157

Chile   The flag of Chile was adopted in 1817, although there were earlier designs. It is clearly based on that of the USA,

158

*166 Cyprus:
national flag*

*167 Czechoslovakia:
national flag*

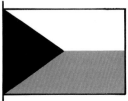

*168 Denmark: national flag
and civil ensign*

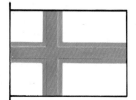

169 Faroe Islands

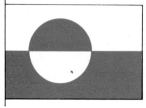

170 Greenland

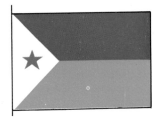

171 Djibouti:
national flag

172 Dominica:
national flag

173 Dominican
Republic:
national flag and
civil ensign

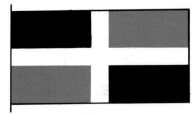

174 Ecuador:
President,
State flag and
naval ensign

which provided inspiration for many American countries in their struggle for political emancipation. The President's flag has the whole arms in the centre of the flag. These have a shield of blue over red with a white star, a crest of three feathers in the national colours; the supporters are a deer and a condor; the motto is *Por la Razon o la Fuerza*, which may be translated as 'By Might or by Right'. This does not appear on the President's flag. The jack is blue with a white star in the centre.

159 **China**   The flag of the Chinese People's Republic was adopted when the people's republic was formed in October 1949. The Communists always used a red flag, and red is the colour which represented the land of China in previous flags. The large gold star stands for the Common Programme of the Communist Party, and the four smaller ones for the four social classes: workers, peasants, petty bourgeoisie, and 'patriotic capitalists'. This is the only national flag of China, apart from the flags of the People's Liberation Army and the Customs Service.

160   **Taiwan** is the headquarters of the Chinese Nationalist government, which uses flags dating from 1928. Their national flag was previously that of the Nationalist party, the Kuo Min Tang, and was the flag of all China until 1949. The red field stands for China, and the blue canton for the heavens, containing a white sun. There is also a civil ensign consisting of the national flag with four zig-zag horizontal stripes in yellow across the red field. The President's standard is red with the white sun on a blue disc in the centre, and a yellow border on all four sides.

Colombia   Colombia is one of three countries which make use of colours introduced in 1806 by Francisco de Miranda: the others are Ecuador and Venezuela. The Colombian flag went
161 through many versions before reaching its present form in 1861. The plain flag is for use on land. At sea a blue oval with a red border and charged with a white star of eight points is added to the centre, to form the civil ensign. The naval ensign

has a white disc with the whole arms in the centre of the flag. The President's flag is similar to this, but with a red border round the disc.

The arms contain a cap of liberty, a pomegranate, and two cornucopiae, and a scene of the isthmus of Panama. The crest is a condor, and the motto is *Libertad y Orden* ('Liberty and Order'). The jack is a blue flag with a white disc containing the arms.

Comoro Islands   The Comoro Islands became independent in July 1975, with a new flag based on the red flags traditionally   162 used in the area. The flag was revised again on 1 October 1978, but still has the crescent and four stars of the original design, which it closely resembles. The four stars stand for the four islands, and the crescent for the Islamic religion.

Congo   Ten years after achieving independence in 1960 Congo transformed itself into a People's Republic, and adopted a red flag with the new national emblem in the canton. This has   163 a crossed hammer and mattock, a wreath of palm leaves, and a large gold star.

Costa Rica   This is one of five states which were once part of the United Provinces of Central America, and its flag is basically the same as that of the confederation (horizontally blue, white,   164 blue), with an additional red stripe. This design dates from 1848. The State flag has the arms on a white oval near the hoist. These show the isthmus of Costa Rica, and five stars for the five former members of the United Provinces. The flag for general use and civil ensign is without the arms.

Cuba   The national flag was designed as early as June 1849,   165 but was not established in Cuba until the country became independent in 1902. It is clearly based on that of the USA, but having only one star it is known as *La Estrella Solitaria* ('The Lone Star', like the flag of Texas). Another historical flag, that

93

175   *Egypt: national flag and civil ensign*

176   *El Salvador: State flag*

177   *Equatorial Guinea: State flag*

178   *Ethiopia: national flag and civil ensign*

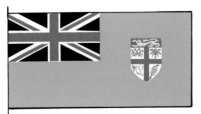

179 Fiji:
national flag

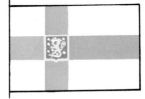

180 Finland:
State flag

181 Åland Islands

182a France: national flag,
civil ensign and jack

of the rebellion of 1868, is now the jack. The President's flag is a blue square with the arms surrounded by six white stars. The arms also date from 1849, and portray Cuba as the key to the Gulf of Mexico.

166 **Cyprus**   The flag of Cyprus, adopted when the island became independent in 1960, is deliberately intended to be neutral, in view of the hostility between the Greek and Turkish populations. It shows a map of the island between two olive branches. In practice the flags of Greece and Turkey only are flown in the south and the north of the island. North Cyprus, a state recognized only by Turkey, has its own white flag with a red crescent and star between two red stripes (below).

167 **Czechoslovakia**   The flag of Czechoslovakia dates from 1920, and combines the colours of Bohemia-Moravia with those of Slovakia, colours which are also expressive of the Pan-Slav liberation movement of the last century. The flag of the President bears the new national emblem, introduced in 1960. This still retains the lion rampant of Bohemia, and the national motto, *Pravda vítezí* ('The truth shall prevail'). On the lion's shoulder is a shield representing Slovakia.

168 **Denmark**   The Danish flag is one of the oldest in continuous

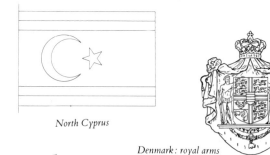

North Cyprus

Denmark: royal arms

96

use in the world. It is one of the most widely used, loved, and respected in its home land. The plain flag is for general civic use, and the form with a triangle cut out of the fly, known as the *splitflag*, is used as the naval ensign and for all official purposes.

The royal standard is the *splitflag* with a square panel in the centre of the cross, charged with the royal arms. These were remarshalled and simplified on the accession of Queen Margrethe in 1972.

The **Faroe Islands**, a dependency of Denmark, have their own arms and flag. The flag, officially adopted in 1948, is of the same pattern as those of other Scandinavian countries, i.e. with the cross slightly off-centre. The colours combine those of the local arms with those of Denmark. 169

The flag of **Greenland** was introduced on 21 June 1985. It is in the Danish colours, and represents the sun rising over the ice-covered land. 170

Djibouti   Formerly the Territory of the Afars and Issas, and before that French Somaliland, this state became independent on 27 June 1977. The flag is based on that of the liberation movement, in which blue stands for the Issas, green for the Afars, white for peace, and the star for unity. 171

Dominica   Before achieving independence on 3 November 1978 Dominica was an Associated State of Britain, and before that a colony. A coat of arms was granted in July 1961 and after November 1965 the flag consisted of the Blue Ensign with the whole arms in the fly. On independence a completely new flag was adopted, but the parrot in the centre of this is taken from the arms. The ten stars stand for the ten parishes of the island. The flag was altered in 1981 so that the cross is now composed of yellow, black, and white pieces and is wider than in the original design. The stance of the parrot has been altered, and the stars are now larger and point away from the centre of 172

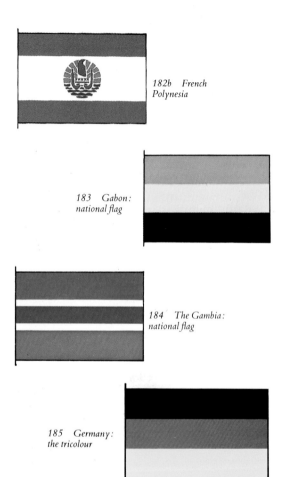

182b French Polynesia

183 Gabon: national flag

184 The Gambia: national flag

185 Germany: the tricolour

186   German Democratic Republic: national flag and civil ensign

187   German Democratic Republic: President

188   German Federal Republic: President

189   Ghana: national flag

the flag. They are green with yellow borders instead of 'lime green' as before. Otherwise the flag remains as adopted on independence.

Dominican Republic   This country was once part of Haiti, and the liberation movement created its flag by placing a white cross over the then flag of Haiti. Later the quarters were re-arranged into the present pattern, and the flag became the national flag in 1844. The State flag has the arms in the centre. The President's flag is white with the State flag in the canton and a large upright yellow anchor in the fly.

Ecuador   Like that of Colombia, the flag of Ecuador is based on the colours of Francisco de Miranda, since the country was part of Colombia until 1830. On secession it was decided to keep the same colours so far as possible, so that the national flags of Ecuador and of Colombia are basically the same. The State flag of Ecuador has the arms in the centre, as do the naval ensign and President's flag. The arms show Mount Chimborazo and a steamer on a lake. The crest is a condor, and the shield is surrounded by national flags, an axe and fasces, and a wreath.

All the provinces of Ecuador have their own flags, as do the **Galapagos Islands** whose flag is horizontally green, white, and blue.

Egypt   From January 1972 Egypt, Libya, and Syria all used the same basic flag to emphasise their unity. The flag, like the present flag of Egypt, was in the red, white, and black colours associated with Arab nationalism and dating back to the Egyptian revolution of 1952. The central emblem was a golden hawk with a blank shield on its breast, and grasping a scroll with the title of the Federation.

Since then Egypt, Libya and Syria have all revised their flags. The flag of Egypt was altered on 4 October 1984 to incorporate the new version of the national emblem. This is not strictly

100

Egypt: national emblem

new since it is the one in use prior to 1971. This is an eagle with a shield on its breast in the national colours, and in its claws a scroll with the name 'Arab Republic of Egypt' in Kufi script. On the flag the emblem is all gold, as was the hawk emblem used by the Federation.

The flag of the President has an extra national emblem in gold in the upper hoist canton. The Army ensign has the shield on the central emblem parted vertically red, white, black, and there are two crossed sabres in the canton. The Navy ensign is the same as the national flag, with two crossed white anchors in the canton.

El Salvador   The flag of El Salvador is basically that of the 176 former United Provinces of Central America, which was re-adopted in 1912. The civil ensign is distinguished from other similar flags by the motto *Dios Union Libertad* ('God, Union, Liberty') in gold letters on the white stripe. The naval ensign has the arms in full colour in the centre of the white stripe. These are also very similar to those of the United Provinces: the five volcanoes stand for the five original members.

Equatorial Guinea   The colours of the national flag, hoisted 177 when independence was achieved in October 1968, represent agricultural resources and the blue sea, with white for peace and red for the struggle for independence. The State flag has the

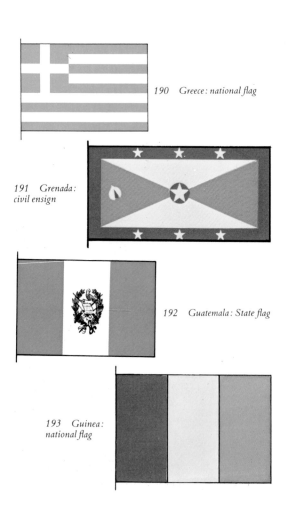

190   Greece: national flag

191   Grenada:
civil ensign

192   Guatemala: State flag

193   Guinea:
national flag

*194   Guinea-Bissau:
national flag*

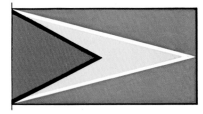

*195   Guyana:
national flag*

*196   Haiti: State flag
and naval ensign*

*197   Honduras:
national flag
and civil ensign*

arms in the centre of the white stripe. These display a silk cotton tree, and six gold stars for the five islands and the mainland. The motto is *Unidad Paz Justicia* ('Unity, Peace, Justice').

Ethiopia The colours of Ethiopia date back to the late nineteenth century and were arranged in their present form in 1904. Before the revolution of 1975 various traditional emblems were added to the tricolour, but the flag for civil use is now the plain one. The official flag adds the new national emblem in the centre, usually shown overlapping the three stripes. In the emblem 14 rays of the sun stand for the 14 divisions of the country, and the inscription at the top reads 'Provisional Military Government of Socialist Ethiopia'.

Fiji: Governor-General

Fiji The flag of Fiji bears the shield from the coat of arms, which dates back to 1908. The shield is quartered by the cross of St George, and is charged with samples of the local vegetation and a flying dove, from the flag of the former kingdom. In chief is an English lion grasping a coconut.

The national flag has a light blue field, the civil ensign a red field, the naval ensign a white field, and the ensign for government vessels a blue one, all following British practice (see p. 33). The flag of the Governor-General is a nearly square blue flag with the royal crest, and the name *Fiji* inscribed on a yellow whale's tooth. These flags all date from the achievement of independence in 1970.

104

Finland The blue and white colours of Finland symbolize the blue lakes and white snowfields of the country. The basic design dates back to 1862, long before Finland achieved independence in 1917. The shape of the cross suggests Finland's affiliation to the Scandinavian countries (see also Sweden p. 157).

The State flag has the shield of arms in the centre of the cross. 180 This shield dates from the sixteenth century, and represents the country in arms overcoming enemies from the east. The ensign is like this but is swallow-tailed with a tongue. The President's flag is like the ensign, but with the cross of the Order of Liberty in the canton.

Åland Islands The flag of these islands, flown only on 181 land, was adopted in 1954. The colours combine those of Finland and Sweden.

France: President

France The Tricolour as we know it today dates from 1794, 182a although the actual colour combination dates from 1789, soon after the fall of the Bastille, and is thought to consist of the colours of Paris—red and blue—combined with the royal colour—white. The Tricolour was first used at sea in 1790, and revised into its present form four years later. The flag for use at sea has stripes of slightly unequal width. Although the Tricolour

*198   Hungary: national flag
and civil ensign*

*199   Iceland: national flag
and civil ensign*

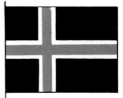

200   India: national flag

201   *India: President*

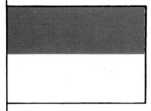

202   *Indonesia: national flag and civil and naval ensign*

203   *Indonesia: President*

is a simple design, it is so effective that it has proved the inspiration of many other red, white, and blue flags in all parts of the world.

The President's flag is a squarish version of the national flag, with his personal emblem in the centre. In the case of the present President this is a blue and gold tree, half an oak and half an olive, symbolising the unity of France. The Prime Minister uses a square national flag with a heavy gold fringe.

Flags for French overseas territories are gradually being 182b introduced. The first to be adopted is that of French Polynesia, which became official on 23 November 1984.

183 **Gabon** The colours of Gabon are another combination of the Pan-African colours with those of France, with which the country is still closely associated. The present design was adopted on independence in August 1960. The President's flag is a square banner of the arms, which show a heraldic ship at sea, with a green chief bearing three gold discs.

184 **The Gambia** The flag of The Gambia represents the river flowing through the green land under the red sunlight, and was adopted on independence in February 1965.

185 **Germany** The German tricolour of black, red, yellow, dates from the early nineteenth century, and was re-adopted by both German republics in 1949. The colours are particularly associated with federal unity. They were first adopted in 1848, and again in 1918, only to be abolished by Hitler in 1933.

German Democratic Republic The plain tricolour was used in East Germany from 1949 to October 1959, when the 186 state emblem was added in the centre. This consists of a hammer and a pair of dividers within a wreath of wheat-ears, bound by a ribbon in the national colours. This is now also the civil ensign.

The naval ensign is red with a band of the national colours across the centre, and on this a red disc with the state emblem contained within a further wreath of golden laurel leaves. The same disc with its charges is placed in the centre of the national flag to form the military ensign.

The President's flag is a square red flag with the state emblem 187 in the centre, and a corded fringe of the national colours.

The former states of East Germany were dissolved in 1954, and their flags are no longer in use there.

German Federal Republic The tricolour was officially adopted in May 1949, and as a national flag is quite plain, unlike that of East Germany. The State flag has the shield of arms in the centre: a yellow shield with the black spread eagle, the ancient emblem of Germany. The naval ensign is like this but swallow-tailed. The President's flag is very similar to that of 188 pre-1933: a square banner of the arms with a red border.

Each of the ten federal states has its own arms and flags, as does West Berlin. Many of these are derived from the emblems of the formerly independent components of Germany.

Baden-Württemberg The flag is black over yellow, and may have the state arms in the centre. It dates from 29 September 1954.

Bavaria The flag is white over blue, or may be blue and white lozenges. Officially adopted on 14 December 1953, but of medieval origin.

Berlin White with red horizontal stripes along the top and bottom edges, and a black rampant bear near the hoist. Officially adopted 26 May 1954 but of older origin.

Bremen Eight horizontal stripes of red and white, with two vertical stripes counterchanged in the hoist. May have the arms on a white panel in the centre. Officially confirmed 21 May 1947, but of medieval origin.

Hamburg Red with a triple towered castle on white in the centre. Of medieval origin, this is a banner of the arms.

Hesse The flag is red over white, and may have the state arms in the centre. Adopted 31 December 1949.

204   Iran: national flag and civil ensign

205   Iraq: national flag

206   Ireland: national flag and civil and naval ensign

207   Ireland: President

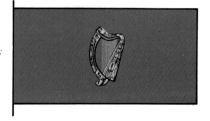

208 *Israel: national flag*

209 *Israel: President*

210 *Italy: national flag*

211 *Italy: naval ensign*

Lower Saxony   The same as the German national flag, but with the state arms in the centre on a large shield. Adopted 17 October 1952.

North Rhine-Westphalia   The flag is red over white over green, and may have the state arms in the centre. Adopted 10 March 1953.

Rhineland-Palatinate   The national tricolour, but with the state arms in the canton. Adopted 15 May 1948.

Saarland   The national tricolour, but with the state arms on a large shield in the centre.

Schleswig-Holstein   Blue over white over red, and may have the state arms in the centre. Adopted 18 January 1957, but older in origin.

189   **Ghana**   The flag of Ghana was the first, after that of Ethiopia, to make use of what are known as the Pan-African colours, and was the first to employ a black star—the 'lodestar of African freedom'. This flag was adopted on independence in March 1957. The civil ensign, naval ensign, and air force ensign, all follow the same pattern as their British counterparts.

Greece   Greece has been a republic since 1973, and all the former royal emblems and flags have been abolished. At one time Greece had two national flags, one plain blue with a white cross and the other with nine horizontal stripes and the white cross in the canton. The first was used inland, and the other at sea, but from June 1975 to December 1978 the plain cross flag was used as the only national flag. This situation has now been reversed and the striped flag is the only national flag for use on 190 land and at sea, although the plain cross flag may still be seen in unofficial use.

The plain cross flag was first adopted in 1822, and the striped flag about ten years later. Its nine stripes are said to stand for the syllables of the national motto *Eleutheria a Thanatos* ('Liberty

112

or Death'). The President's flag is plain blue with the arms in the centre.

Grenada   Adopted on independence in February 1974 the flag of Grenada illustrates the island's principal product, the nutmeg. The seven stars represent the seven parishes of the island. The colours represent sunshine (yellow), agricultural wealth (green), and the friendly spirit of the people (red). The flag for use on land is in the proportions 3:5, and for use at sea 1:2. 191

Guatemala   Guatemala uses the colours of Central America but arranged vertically. This design dates from 1871, following several earlier versions. The plain flag is the national flag and civil ensign. The State flag has the arms in the centre, these consist of a scroll with the original date of independence, and a red and green quetzal bird. 192

Guinea   Guinea adopted the same colours as those of Ghana, on achieving independence in October 1958, but arranged in the same style as in the French tricolour. This pattern was derived from the flag of the dominant political party, which made use of the Pan-African colours. 193

Guinea-Bissau   This country also uses the Pan-African colours, and a black star as in the flag of Ghana. This had been in use since 1961 by the liberation movement. The flag was adopted on independence in September 1973. 194

Guyana   The colours of Guyana are not the Pan-African colours, but represent the green forests, the golden future, and the national spirit (red), perseverance (black), and the country's rivers (white). On land the flag has the proportions 3:5, and at sea 1:2. The flag was adopted on independence in May 1966. The President's flag is a square banner of the arms, which have 195

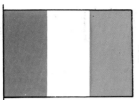

*212   Ivory Coast:
national flag*

*213   Jamaica: national
flag and civil ensign*

*214   Japan: national flag
and civil ensign*

215   Japan: Emperor

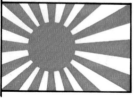

216   Japan: naval ensign

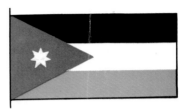

*217   Jordan:
national flag*

218   Kampuchea: national flag

219   Kenya: national flag

220   Kiribati: national flag

*221   Republic of Korea:
national flag*

blue wavy lines, a Victoria lily, a pheasant, and a green inescutcheon charged with a crown of feathers.

Haiti The traditional blue and red flag of Haiti was restored on 25 February 1986 after the overthrow of the Duvalier régime. This flag, which dates from the war of independence in 1803, had been replaced in 1964 by the rival black and red version with the strips arranged vertically. The arms in this version were without the Cap of Liberty at the top of the palm-tree, but this has now been restored. The flag with the arms is the 'Official Flag' for use by the President and the Government; without the arms it is for civil use on land and sea.

Honduras The flag of Honduras is very similar to that of the United Provinces of Central America. The five stars represent the five original members. The flag with stars is the national flag and civil ensign. The State flag and naval ensign has the national emblem in the centre. This consists of a pyramid rising from the sea within an oval with the legend *Libre Soberana Independiente* ('Free, Sovereign, Independent'); this is surrounded by two cornucopiae and a landscape strewn with allegorical items.

Hungary The colours of Hungary are based on those of the ancient coat of arms. The flag came into use in 1848, with the coat of arms in the centre. In 1949 the arms were replaced by the emblem of the People's Republic. Following the revolution of 1956 the emblem was removed, and the flag is now plain.

Iceland The colours of Iceland are a combination of those of its old coat of arms and those of Denmark, and are also those of Norway. The flag dates from 1913 and was officially established in 1918. It became that of the independent republic in June 1944. The naval ensign is like the national flag, but with a swallow-tail. The President's flag is like the ensign, but with a white panel in the centre of the cross, bearing the coat of arms. The shield dates from 1919, but is now supported by creatures from ancient Norse myth.

India The flag of India was originally that of the Indian 200
National Congress, with a blue Buddhist emblem, known as
the *chakra*, added on independence in August 1947. The colours
represent renunciation, peace and Nature. The civil ensign and
naval ensign are of the same pattern as those of the UK (see
p. 33).

The President's flag is quartered blue and red, charged with 201
the state emblem in the first quarter, the Lions of Asoka; then
an elephant outlined in yellow, a pair of scales, and a bowl of
lotus blossoms.

Indonesia The colours of Indonesia date back to the medieval
empire that flourished in this area. The flag was introduced in 202
1945 and became that of the independent republic in December
1949. The jack is the flag of the pre-war independence
movement. The President's flag is in yellow (the 'royal' colour), 203
and is charged with a gold star within a wreath of rice and
cotton.

Iran The flag of Iran developed slowly over several centuries,
and for over a century bore the well-known lion and sun
emblem. The tricolour form was adopted in 1907, and was at 204
first very long and with unusual shades of colour. In April 1980
Iran became an Islamic Republic, and a new version of the
national flag was adopted, containing the new national emblem
in red in the centre, in place of the crowned lion and sun. It also
has the inscription *Allah Akbar* repeated 22 times along the
edges of the red and green stripes. This symbolises the date *22
Bahman 1358* (=11 February 1979) when the Ayatollah
Khomeini returned to Iran.

Iraq The present national flag dates from 1963, and is based 205
on that of the former United Arab Republic. The three stars
stand for the union it was intended to effect with Egypt and
Syria. The colours are those of the Arab liberation movement
(see p. 12).

222 Korean People's Democratic Republic: national flag

223 Kuwait: national flag

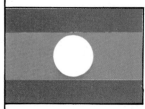

224 Laos: national flag

225 Lebanon: national flag

226 Lesotho:
national flag

227 Liberia: national
flag and civil ensign

228 Libya: national flag

229 Liechtenstein:
national flag

230 Luxembourg:
national flag

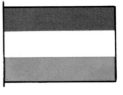

119

206 **Ireland** The Irish Tricolour dates from 1848. The colours symbolize the Protestants (orange) and the Catholics (green), and the peace resulting from a united Ireland. It was adopted by the Irish Free State in 1920.

207 The President's flag features the ancient harp of Brian Boru, which is also found in British royal heraldry. The jack is green, with the same harp in yellow. This flag ('The Green Flag'), was the earliest symbol of the Home Rule movement.

208 **Israel** The flag of Israel dates back to the earliest days of Zionism. Its central emblem is the *Magen David* ('Shield of David'), and the blue and white stripes are taken from the Hebrew *tallith*, or prayer-shawl. It was adopted when Israel became independent in May 1948. The civil ensign is also blue,

209 with the *Magen David* on a white oval. The President's flag is a banner of the arms, which employ the *menorah*, the seven-branched candlestick which once stood in the Temple of Jerusalem. Around this is a wreath of olive, and underneath the name 'Israel' in Hebrew.

210 **Italy** The Italian Tricolour has its origin in Napoleon's liberation of the 1790s, and it is probable that the design is based on that of France. The flag did not become permanent until 1848, and did not become that of a united Italy until 1861.

In 1946 the arms of Savoy were removed from the centre, and the flag is now quite plain. New civil and naval ensigns were introduced at that time, with a new shield in the centre.

211 The shield contains the arms of Venice, Genoa, Amalfi, and Pisa, but the quarter for Venice is slightly different in the naval ensign from that in the civil ensign. The jack is a banner of the arms as in the naval ensign.

212 **Ivory Coast** The flag was introduced in 1959, and is probably based on that of France. A variety of meanings are attached to the colours.

Jamaica   The flag was adopted on independence in August   213
1962. The colours stand for the agricultural and mineral wealth
of the island and the hardships facing its people. The royal flag
is a banner of the arms with the royal cypher in the centre. The
naval ensign is like that of Britain (p. 33), with the national flag
in the canton. The Governor-General's flag is royal blue with
the royal crest and the name *Jamaica* on a gold scroll.

Japan   The red sun on the flag of Japan represents the 'land of   214
the rising sun', and is known as a *mon*, a purely Japanese heraldic
form. The chrysanthemum on the royal standard is also a *mon*,   215
and forms the national emblem. The naval ensign is the same as   216
that used before the Second World War, and was restored to
use in 1954.

Jordan   The flag of Jordan is derived from that used in the
first Arab revolt of 1917 and the colours are known as the Pan-   217
Arab colours (see p. 12). The seven-pointed star was added to
distinguish the flag from that then used in the Hedjaz, and its
points stand for the basic tenets of the Moslem faith. Without
the star this flag is used by the protagonists of Arab Palestine.

The naval ensign is white with the national flag in the canton
and the combined services emblem in the fly in black. The
royal standard is a complicated flag of pieces in the Arab colours
and the national flag in the centre, but with a crown in place of
the star.

Kampuchea   The new regime which took over in January
1979 adopted a new form of the national flag, in which the
temple has five towers and is stylised in a new way. The former   218
flag (temple with three towers) is still in use by the displaced
regime.

Kenya   Introduced when Kenya became independent in   219
December 1963, the colours of the flag are based on those of the
dominant political party, and are also those of the 'Black

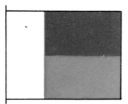

231 Madagascar:
national flag

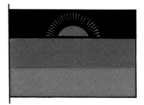

232 Malawi: national flag

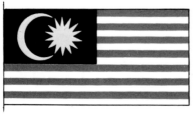

233 Malaysia:
national flag
and civil ensign

234 Maldive Islands:
national flag

235   Mali: national flag

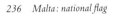

236   Malta: national flag

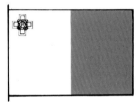

237   Mauritania:
national flag

238   Mauritius: national flag

Liberation' movement. The red in this case is a special shade known as 'Kenya red'. The naval ensign is white with the national flag in the canton and a red vertical anchor in the fly.

Kiribati The former Gilbert Islands became independent under this name in July 1979, and adopted a flag based on the 220 coat of arms. The coat of arms of the then Gilbert and Ellice Islands was granted in 1937, and the shield was used as an ensign badge until the independence of the Gilbert Islands. The Ellice Islands, now known as Tuvalu, became a separate colony in 1975.

221 **Korea, Republic of** The strange devices on the flag of South Korea are: in the centre the *yang-yin* and around it four *kwae* symbols. The first represents the union of opposites, and the latter the four seasons, the four winds, etc. This flag was adopted in January 1950, but is based on that used by Korea before 1910.

222 **Korean People's Democratic Republic** This flag was adopted in September 1948 for the republic formed at that time in North Korea. The colours are the same as those of the original Korean flag but in a new Communist pattern.

223 **Kuwait** A new flag was adopted by Kuwait when independence was achieved in November 1961. The colours are the Pan-Arab colours (p. 12).

Laos Laos became a Communist republic in December 1975, 224 and the flag of the Pathet Lao was adopted. The blue stripe is said to represent the Mekong River, the disc the moon, and the red the unity of purpose of the Laos and the Vietnamese.

Lebanon The cedar tree has been the symbol of the Lebanon since Biblical times. It was placed on the present flag in December 1943 when the country became independent. The 225 red and white colours are probably derived from those of the Lebanese Legion in the First World War.

Lesotho   The strange object on the flag of Lesotho is a straw   226
hat! This is the typical national head-gear. The flag was adopted
in October 1966, in the colours of the dominant political party.
However, a year after the coup d'état of 20 January 1986 a new
national flag has been adopted.

Liberia   The flag of Liberia is clearly based on that of the   227
USA, from whence most of its immigrants came, except that it
has only eleven stripes and one white star. It was adopted on
independence in July 1847. The largest single number of
merchant ships in the world sail under this flag.

   The flag of the President is square and blue with the stripes
from the national flag arranged vertically on a shield with a
blue chief with one white star and a gold border. In each canton
is a white star. The jack is blue with a single white star.

Libya: national emblem

Libya   Libya was a founder-member of the Federation of
Arab Republics in 1972, but broke away in 1977 when Egypt
began peace negotiations with Israel. From then on a plain
green flag has been in use, symbolising the 'Green Revolution'.   228
The national emblem has been altered to include a green shield
on the falcon's breast and the title 'Libyan Arab Republic' on
the scroll.

Liechtenstein   The colours of Liechtenstein date back to the   229
early nineteenth century. The coronet was added in 1937 to
avoid confusion with the then flag of Haiti. The royal standard

239   Mexico:
national flag and
civil and naval ensign

240   Monaco: national flag

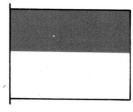

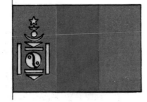

241   Mongolia: national flag

242   Morocco: national flag

243   Mozambique:
national flag

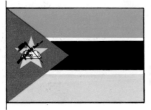

244   Nauru:
national flag

245   Nepal: national flag

246   Netherlands:
national flag and
civil and naval ensign

247   Netherlands: jack

248   Netherlands: royal standard

127

is a plain horizontal bicolour of yellow over red, which makes it a banner of the royal arms.

Luxembourg   The colours of Luxembourg are derived from the coat of arms, which is like the civil ensign, having blue and white stripes with a red lion rampant over all. The blue is usually a shade lighter than in the flag of the Netherlands. The national flag can further be distinguished from that of the Netherlands by its ratio, which is 3:5 rather than 2:3.

The present standard of the Grand Duke was adopted soon after his accession in 1964. It has a blue field with golden billets, from the arms of the House of Orange-Nassau, and the shield of Luxembourg within the collar of the Order of the Oaken Crown.

Madagascar   When Madagascar was an independent kingdom its flags were all red and white. Green was added when the republic was formed in 1958. Red and white are said to stand for the Hova people, and green for the coastal inhabitants.

Malawi   The flag of Malawi was adopted on independence in July 1964, on the basis of the flag of the dominant political party, and uses the Black Liberation colours (see Kenya p. 121). The red sun is from the old arms of Nyasaland. The President's flag is red with the gold lion passant from the arms, and a scroll with the name *Malawi* in black letters.

Malaysia   The stripes of the national flag stand for the members of the federation and for the Federal District, as do the points of the star in the canton. The flag was adopted in September 1963 on the basis of that of Malaya. The civil ensign is red with the national flag fimbriated blue (i.e. with a blue border) in the canton. The naval ensign is white with the national flag in the canton and the combined services emblem in the fly in blue.

All the states of Malaysia have their own arms and flags.

Maldive Islands   The flag of the Maldives has evolved over 234 a number of years from a plain red one. The present design was adopted in July 1965. The flag of the Head of State has a crescent as well as a star in the centre.

Mali   The colours of Mali are the Pan-African colours 235 arranged in the same form as the French Tricolour. The flag was adopted when the country became independent in September 1960.

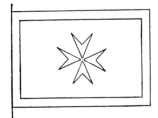

Malta: civil ensign

Malta   The flag of Malta is of considerable antiquity, being 236 derived from the colours of the arms of the Knights of St John. The cross of the George Cross was added in 1943 on a small blue canton, which was removed on independence in September 1964. The civil ensign employs the badge of the Order of St John, the well-known 'Maltese Cross'.

Mauritania   The flag of Mauritania was adopted in April 237 1959 and the Moslem star and crescent moon express the country's official title: the Islamic Republic of Mauritania.

Mauritius   The colours of the flag are derived from the coat 238 of arms, but are capable of several interpretations. The flag was adopted on independence in March 1968. The civil ensign is red with the national flag in the canton and the arms on a white disc in the fly.

249   Netherlands Antilles

250   Aruba

251   Bonaire

252   Curacao

253   New Zealand:
national flag and jack

254   New Zealand:
Queen's personal flag

255
Cook Islands

256   Niue

257   Nicaragua:
national flag and
civil and naval
ensign

239 **Mexico**   The emblem on the flag of Mexico is the old Aztec symbol for Mexico City, formerly Tenochtitlán, where, according to legend, the wandering Aztecs found an eagle grasping a snake whilst standing on a cactus on an island in the middle of a lake. The colours of the flag derive from a flag used in the independence movement of the 1820s, standing for independence, unity, and religion. The central emblem has varied over the years: the present form was established in September 1968. The same flag serves as President's standard, national flag, and civil and naval ensign.

240 **Monaco**   The colours of the flag are derived from the arms of the principality, which are of medieval origin. The present form of the flag was adopted in 1881. The Prince's standard is white with the whole arms in the centre. The national flag may be distinguished from that of Indonesia by its ratio—4:5 compared with 2:3.

241 **Mongolia**   The blue in the flag of Mongolia is the particular colour of the Mongols, whilst red stands for revolution. The emblem in the hoist is the *soyonbo*, a combination of various abstract devices surmounted by the gold star of communism. The present design was adopted in February 1949.

242 **Morocco**   The flag of Morocco dates from 1915, when the green pentacle, or 'Solomon's Seal', was added to the previously plain red flag. Morocco regained its independence in 1956 and retained the already-established flag. The naval ensign adds the royal crown in gold in the canton.

243 **Mozambique**   A new design for the national flag was adopted in April 1983, which reverts to the form of the flag of the liberation movement Frelimo and replaces the flag adopted on independence in 1975. In the red triangle is a gold star charted with a crossed rifle and mattock surmounting an open book. These elements are taken from the national emblem.

Nauru   This island lies just south of the Equator, as expressed by the design of its flag. The star represents the island, and the 244 twelve points its twelve native tribes. The flag was adopted on independence in January 1968.

Nepal   This is the only national flag that is not rectangular. 245 The design was streamlined in December 1962 but still retains the emblems of the sun and the moon.

Netherlands   The flag of the Netherlands derives from the 246 colours of William of Orange who led the independence movement in the sixteenth century. The top stripe was originally orange, forming a flag called the *Prinsvlag*, but became red about 1650. The jack also dates back to those critical 247 years, being based on the flag used by the States-General. The royal standard has the Dutch lion in the centre, and the bugles 248 of Orange-Nassau in the cantons. The standard of Prince Claus is blue with an orange cross, and has a Dutch lion in the first and fourth quarters and a white castle in the others. All the royal standards employ the traditional blue, white and orange colours.

All eleven provinces of the Netherlands have their own arms and flags, as do most of the cities and communes.

Netherlands Antilles   The flag is based on that of the 249 Netherlands, and dates from 2 December 1959. At that time the blue band contained six white stars to stand for the six Dutch dependencies in the West Indies, but on 20 March 1986 the stars were reduced to five, following the promotion of Aruba to self-governing status. **Aruba** has a flag adopted in 250 1976. **Bonaire** has a flag adopted in 1981. The flag of **Curaçao** 251 was adopted in 1984. **Saba**: The island flag was the winning 252 design in a competition and was adopted on 6 December 1985. **St Maarten**: The flag was introduced on 13 June 1985, and contains the whole arms adopted on 17 November 1982. Only the island of St Eustatius is now without a flag.

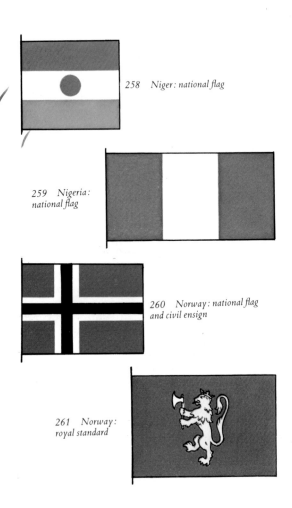

258   Niger: national flag

259   Nigeria:
national flag

260   Norway: national flag
and civil ensign

261   Norway:
royal standard

134

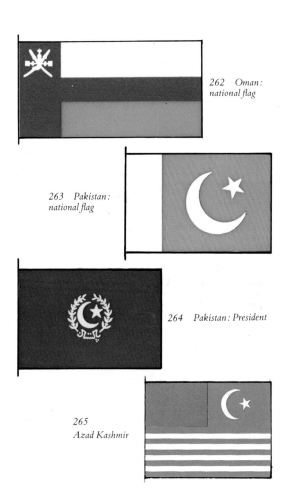

262 Oman:
national flag

263 Pakistan:
national flag

264 Pakistan: President

265
Azad Kashmir

253 **New Zealand**   New Zealand became independent in 1917, but kept the flag adopted in 1869. This is very similar to that of Australia, but has only four stars of the Southern Cross, and these are red with white borders. The civil ensign is red with
254 white stars and the naval ensign white with red stars. The royal flag is a banner of the arms with the royal cypher in the centre. The Air Force ensign is that of the UK (see p. 36) with the letters NZ in the centre of the roundel. The civil air ensign is also like that of the UK (p. 37), with the red stars, edged white, in the lower fly canton.

Cook Islands   These are a self-governing dependency of
255 New Zealand. A new version for local use was introduced in August 1979. It has a ring of fifteen stars, one for each island.

256 **Niue**   The flag of Niue, also a self-governing dependency, was adopted in October 1975. The bright yellow field stands for the warmth of friendship between Niue and New Zealand.

257 **Nicaragua**   The national flag is identical to that of the United Provinces of Central America of 1823–39, to which Nicaragua once belonged. The national arms which appear in the centre of the State flag and ensign are very similar to those of the United Provinces. The present form of the flags dates from 1908.

258 **Niger**   The orange disc in the centre represents the sun, the orange stripe the Sahara desert, and the green stripe the grasslands, divided by the white river. This flag was adopted in November 1959, prior to independence in 1960.

259 **Nigeria**   The green in the flag of Nigeria represents the green land of the country, and the white is for peace. The flag was adopted on independence in October 1960. The naval ensign is like that of the UK but with the flag of Nigeria in the canton.

260 **Norway**   The flag of Norway was first adopted in 1821, but was not brought into general use until 1898. It is derived from that of Denmark, to which Norway once belonged. The naval

ensign is swallow-tailed with a tongue, one of the few of this
shape still in use. The royal standard is a banner of the arms,
which show the ancient lion of Norway grasping the axe of St
Olav. The Crown Prince's is the same, but swallow-tailed.

Oman   For several centuries Oman used a plain red flag, but
in December 1970 a new range of flags was introduced, using
the state emblem in the canton. The national flag also adds
white and green panels to the original red. The emblem is a
native dagger crossed by two sabres and three links of a chain.
The Sultan's standard is red with a green frame in the centre,
containing the national emblem ensigned with the royal crown,
all in gold. The naval ensign is blue with the national flag in the
canton and a white upright foul anchor in the fly.

Pakistan   Like that of India, the flag of Pakistan is based on
that of the principal independence movement, in this case the
Moslem League. The white vertical strip was added on
independence in August 1947 to represent non-Moslems. The
civil ensign is red with the national flag in the canton. The
naval ensign is like the national flag, but has the ratio 1 : 2 rather
than 2 : 3. The President's flag is blue with a yellow crescent and
star within a wreath, and the name 'Pakistan', also in yellow, in
the centre. The jack is blue with the navy badge in the centre in
white.
    Azad Kashmir is that part of Kashmir occupied by Pakistan.
The orange panel on its flag stands for the Hindu population,
next to the emblem of the Moslem League.

Panama   Based on that of the USA the flag of Panama was
adopted in December 1903, when the country broke away
from Colombia. The colours are said to represent the Liberals
and the Conservatives. The flag is also used in the Panama Canal
Zone.

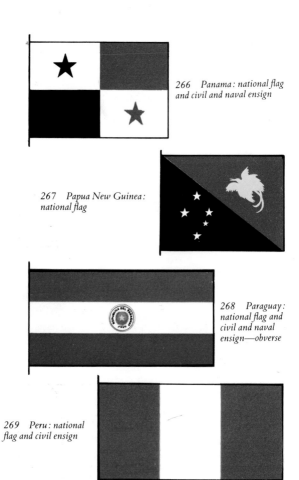

266 *Panama: national flag and civil and naval ensign*

267 *Papua New Guinea: national flag*

268 *Paraguay: national flag and civil and naval ensign—obverse*

269 *Peru: national flag and civil ensign*

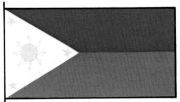

270 *Philippines:*
national flag

271 *Philippines: President*

272 *Poland:*
national flag

273 *Portugal: national flag*
and civil and naval ensign

267 **Papua New Guinea** The flag of Papua New Guinea was
adopted in March 1971, prior to independence in September
1975. It was designed by a local art teacher, and combines the
traditional emblem of New Guinea, the bird of paradise, with
the Southern Cross of Australia.

Paraguay: national arms   Paraguay: Treasury Seal

268 **Paraguay** Paraguay is one of the few countries to have a
national flag with a different design on each side. The difference
lies in the central emblems, as shown. The obverse has the
national arms in the centre, and the reverse the Treasury Seal.
The present design of the national flag dates from 1842, but is
based on earlier designs going back to 1812. The President's
flag is blue, with the state emblem (without the title), in the
centre, and a gold star in each canton. The jack is a square white
flag with a gold star (known as the 'Star of May') in the centre
of a saltire of red and blue arms.

269 **Peru** The red and white colours of Peru date back to 1820
when José de San Martin liberated the country. Flags with
various designs in these colours were used until 1825 when the
present design was adopted. The President's flag is white with
the whole national arms in the centre, and a gold Inca sun in
each canton. The naval ensign is like the national flag, with a
simplified version of the national arms in the centre. The jack is

Peru: whole arms   *Peru: simplified arms*

white and square, with a red border all round and the simplified arms in the centre.

Philippines The Philippine flag was adopted during the struggle for independence against the Spanish in the 1890s. The flag was made official in 1919, and was adopted as that of the independent republic in July 1946. The colours are probably derived from those of the USA. The three small stars stand for the three main island groups. The sun is the 'Sun of Liberty', and its eight rays stand for the eight provinces where the rebellion began. 270

The President's flag is blue with the state badge in the centre, within a ring of fifty-one stars. The jack is blue with the sun and stars as in the national flag. 271

Poland The colours of the Polish flag are derived from the national emblem, a white eagle on a red field. This in turn dates back to at least 1241. A crown, which originally appeared on the eagle's head, was removed by the post-war government. The flag was re-established in 1918 when the country's independence was restored. The plain flag is the national flag. The civil ensign has the shield in the centre of the white stripe. The naval ensign is like this but the flag is swallow-tailed. The 272

141

274   Qatar:
national flag

275   Romania: national flag
and civil and naval ensign

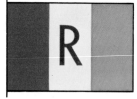

276   Rwanda: national flag

277   St Kitts-Nevis

278   St Lucia:
national flag

*279   St Vincent
and the Grenadines:
national flag*

*280   San Marino:
State flag*

*281   São Tomé
and Principe:
national flag*

*282   Sa'udi Arabia:
national flag—obverse*

283   Senegal: national flag

143

President's flag, a banner of the arms, is no longer in use. The jack is square, white over red with a counterchanged cross pattée charged with a red disc bearing an arm and sword: an emblem derived from medieval Polish flags.

273 **Portugal** The central device on the flag of Portugal has remained unchanged for centuries: the white shield with five smaller shields (the *quinas*) and a red border with seven gold castles. The *quinas* reputedly date back to 1139. The 'Bordure of Castile' was added in 1252, and the armillary sphere in 1815. The latter represents Portugal's rôle in early voyages of discovery. The colours were adopted in the revolution of 1910: they were previously blue and white. The President's flag is green with the emblem from the national flag in the centre. The jack is a red field with a green border, and is charged with the same emblem.

Qatar Originally the flag of Qatar was ordinary red, but sun and sea turned it to the present maroon colour, which is now
274 official. The flag, dating back to about 1855, was retained when the country became independent in September 1971.

Romania Blue, yellow, and red are colours derived from the arms of the provinces which united to form Romania in 1861. The national arms have always appeared in the centre of the flag. The present emblem was introduced in 1948, and amended
275 in 1965. Also since that date the national flag has been the same as the civil ensign, which did not previously have the central emblem. It is now also the naval ensign.
The jack is square with a blue field charged with a red saltire fimbriated yellow, and the arms over all in the centre. The President and other ministers have a square version of the national flag with a border of white and red, and the arms over all in the centre.

276 **Rwanda** The letter R on the flag of Rwanda was added when the country became independent in July 1962, to distinguish it

from that of Guinea. The colours are the Pan-African colours, chosen by the dominant political party.

Saint Kitts-Nevis   These islands became independent on 19 September 1983 with a new flag and coat of arms. The flag was 277 the winning entry in a local competition. The two stars do not stand for the two islands but for hope and liberty. The previous flag, adopted 27 February 1967, represented the three islands of St Kitts-Nevis-Anguilla, but Anguilla having seceded from the group remains a separate British dependency (see page 44).

St Lucia   This island became independent of the United Kingdom on 22 February 1979, but the only change made to the flag adopted in March 1967 was to alter the proportions. 278 Originally the flag was 5:8 but its shape is now 1:2. The central emblem can be interpreted as the volcanic peaks of the Pitons rising from the golden sands amid the blue sea.

St Vincent and the Grenadines   These islands became independent on 27 November 1979 with a flag of vertical blue, yellow, and green vertical stripes containing the whole coat of arms on a stylised breadfruit leaf in the centre, and with white borders to the yellow strip. However, on 21 October 1985 a new version of the flag was introduced. This omits the white 279 fimbriation, and replaces the coat of arms and leaf with three green diamonds, expressive of the state's nickname: 'the Gem of the Antilles'.

San Marino   Possibly the oldest state in Europe with a continuous history of independence, San Marino has a flag in 280 colours derived from its arms, which portray three towers on a blue field. The general flag is plain, but the State flag has the arms over all in the centre.

São Tomé and Principe   The two stars stand for the two 281 islands, on a flag in the Pan-African colours. Before independence

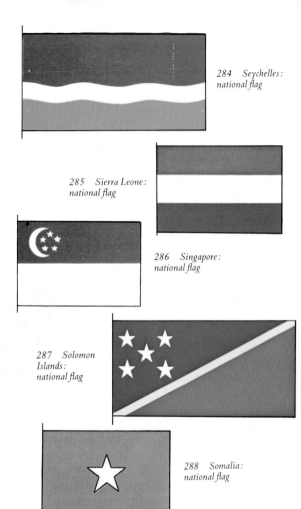

284 Seychelles:
national flag

285 Sierra Leone:
national flag

286 Singapore:
national flag

287 Solomon
Islands:
national flag

288 Somalia:
national flag

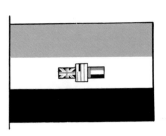

*289   South Africa:
national flag and civil ensign*

290   Transkei

291   Bophuthatswana

292   Ciskei

293   Venda

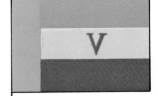

in July 1975 the liberation movement used the same flag but with stripes of equal width.

282 **Sa'udi Arabia**   The inscription on the flag of Sa'udi Arabia is the *shahada*, the Moslem statement of faith: 'There is no God but Allah, and Mohammed is the Prophet of Allah.' The green is the colour of the Wahabi sect. This is the only national flag where the charge on the reverse side is not a mirror-image of the obverse. This is achieved by sewing two copies of the flag together. The royal flag is the same design, but has the national emblem in gold in the lower fly canton.

283 **Senegal**   The green star on the flag of Senegal distinguishes it from that of Mali, a country to which Senegal was joined when they achieved independence in 1960. The flag then had a black ideogram called the *kanaga* in the centre, but when Senegal seceded in August of that year this emblem was replaced by the green star, taken from Senegal's coat of arms.

Seychelles   These islands became independent in June 1976, but altered their flag just one year later, following a bloodless
284 coup d'état. The present national flag is based on that of the currently dominant political party. The President's flag is the same design but has a white disc in the centre bearing the coat of arms.

285 **Sierra Leone**   The flag was adopted on independence in April 1961, and employs colours found in the coat of arms.

Singapore   Red and white are colours often used in south-east Asia, and the flag of Singapore is only distinguished from
286 that of Indonesia by the crescent and stars. The flag was originally adopted when Singapore was a crown colony, in 1959, and was retained when it seceded from Malaysia in August 1965. The civil ensign is all red with the crescent and stars within a ring, all in white in the centre. The President's

*Singapore:
civil ensign*

flag is red with the crescent and stars in large proportions. The naval ensign is white with the President's flag in the canton and a red and white compass rose in the fly.

Solomon Islands   These islands became independent in July 1978 and adopted a flag granted the previous November. The colours are said to represent the green land, the sun and the rivers. The five stars stand for the five districts. The flag of the Governor-General is unusual in that the title is written on an outline frigate bird instead of the usual scroll (see p. 73). The Solomon Islands have a full range of ensigns: the civil ensign is red with the national flag in the canton. There is also a new coat of arms.

Somalia   This flag was adopted in October 1954, when Somalia was under United Nations aegis, and the colours and general design are based on the UN flag. The five points of the star are said to stand for the five areas where Somalis live. The flag was retained on independence in July 1960.

South Africa   It is no coincidence that the flags of South Africa are like those of the Netherlands, since they have a common origin in the *Prinsvlag* (see p. 133). The national flag dates from May 1928, and is intended to represent the English

South Africa: President

149

294　Spain: national
flag and civil ensign

295　Sri Lanka:
national flag

296　Sri Lanka:
President's flag

297　Sudan:
national flag

298   Surinam: national
flag and civil ensign

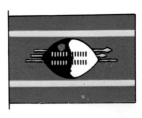

299   Swaziland:
national flag

300   Sweden: national
flag and civil ensign

301   Switzerland:
national flag

302   Syria: national
flag

and Afrikaner elements in the population. The small flags in the centre are the Union Jack, for the two British colonies of the Cape and Natal, and the flags of the former Boer republics of the Orange Free State (in the centre) and the Transvaal. The *Prinsvlag*, or 'Van Riebeeck Flag' as it is known in South Africa, was chosen to commemorate the colonization of South Africa by the Dutch in the early seventeenth century under Jan van Riebeeck. This design became the civil ensign and jack in 1951 and was retained when South Africa became a republic in May 1961. A new flag for the State President was adopted on 14 September 1984, consisting of the national colours arranged to form a white triangle based on the hoist. In its centre is the national coat of arms with the letters S.P. above it. The previous flag was blue with the arms and initials in the centre. The naval ensign is white with a green Scandinavian cross, and the national flag, fimbriated white, in the canton.

·· The flags of the Orange Free State and of the Transvaal are still in use, and there are also flags for the 'homelands' established for the African population. Four of these are regarded as independent by South Africa: **Bophuthatswana** (1977), **Ciskei** (1981), **Transkei** (1976), and **Venda** (1979). Their flags were all adopted prior to independence (dates in brackets). There are also 'homelands' in Namibia, a territory occupied by South Africa and which otherwise has no distinctive flag.

Spain   The basic form of the national flag of Spain dates from 1785, but the current pattern was only established at the end of the civil war in 1939, although it had been used on the Nationalist side since August 1936. The republican flag, used 1931–9, had three equal horizontal stripes of red, yellow, and purple. These colours are derived from the arms of Castile and León, which may be seen as the two upper quarters in the jack. The two lower quarters in the jack are for Aragon and Navarre.

The coat of arms, which appears on the state and government flags, dates in its present form from December 1981, although

Spain: arms

Spain: royal standard

the quarters are all of ancient origin. They represent the ancient kingdoms of Castile, León, Aragon, Navarre, and Granada. The shield also contains the badge of the house of Bourbon (three gold fleurs de lis on a blue oval) and is supported by the Pillars of Hercules.

The Royal Standard was adopted in April 1971 and has the shield supported by the 'saltire raguly' of Burgundy and the chain of the Order of the Golden Fleece. This is all in full colour on a blue field.

All the regions of Spain have flags, although some are only provisional. Among the best-known are those of the **Basque Lands** (red with a green saltire surmounted by a white cross), **Catalonia** (nine horizontal stripes of yellow and red), **Galicia** (white with a blue diagonal band), and the **Canary Islands** (vertically white, blue, yellow).

Sri Lanka   The core of the flag of Sri Lanka is the dark red 295 field with the lion and sword. This is based on the flag of Kandy, the central kingdom of Ceylon. This flag was adopted on the independence of Ceylon in February 1948. In 1951 the orange and green panels were added, representing the Tamil and Moslem minority groups. In May 1972 the country became a republic, and the devices in the cantons were altered to represent the leaves of the *bo* tree. The national arms were also altered at

303 Tanzania: national flag

304 Thailand: national flag and civil ensign

305 Togo: national flag

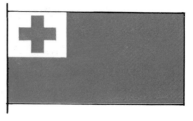

306 Tonga: national flag and civil ensign

154

307 Trinidad and
Tobago: national flag

308 Tunisia: national flag

309 Turkey: national flag

310 Tuvalu:
national flag

296 this time, and a flag was introduced for the President. This was altered in 1978 to the present design, and the shape of the *bo* leaves on the national flag was also slightly altered at this time.

The civil ensign is red with the national flag in the canton. The naval ensign is like that of the UK (see p. 36), with the Sri Lanka flag in the canton.

Sudan The colours of the flag of the Sudan are those common to most Arab countries, although a variety of meanings are
297 attributed to them. The present design was adopted in May 1970, and replaced the first national flag, which was horizontally blue, yellow, and green, and which had been adopted on independence in January 1956. The President's flag is like the national flag but with the arms in the centre of the white stripe.

Surinam Surinam became independent in November 1975
298 and adopted a flag based on those of the main political parties. The coat of arms has remained basically the same as that introduced in December 1959. The arms are added on a square white panel, replacing the star on the national flag, to form the President's flag.

299 **Swaziland** The flag of Swaziland was adopted on independence in October 1967. It is based on that of the Swazi Pioneer Corps which served in the British Army in the Second World War. The shield etc. date back to 1890 when the country was previously independent. The staff and shield bear tassels of widowbird and lourie feathers, an ornamentation reserved for the King. The shield is that of the Emasotsha regiment.

The royal standard is the same as the national flag, but has a small gold lion in the top blue stripe, facing the fly; this dates from September 1968.

Sweden The colours of Sweden are derived from the national
300 arms: three gold crowns on blue. The flag dates from the mid-sixteenth century. The special 'Scandinavian' form of the flag dates from 1665, and it is similar to that used in neighbouring

Sweden: Greater State Arms

countries. The distinctive form of the naval ensign, swallow-tailed with a tongue, is also particularly Scandinavian.

The royal standard is like the naval ensign, with a white panel in the centre of the cross charged with the whole arms, known as the Greater State Arms. Other members of the royal family have a similar flag, but charged with the Lesser State Arms. There is also a royal pennant of blue over yellow, with the Greater Arms on a white field in the chief. This can be used in conjunction with either of the standards.

The jack is the same as the ensign. The flag of the Minister of Defence is square, divided vertically blue and yellow. On the blue are three crowns, and on the yellow a blue upright sword. The Supreme Commander has a square flag divided blue over yellow horizontally. On the blue are the three crowns, and on the yellow two crossed blue and gold batons. The King's personal flag is a square banner of the royal arms.

The flag of **Scania** (*Skåne*) in southern Sweden is like the national flag, but yellow on red.

Switzerland   Although Switzerland is an old country its flag is of comparatively recent adoption. The white 'couped' cross is an old emblem, originally that of Schwyz, one of the three 301 original cantons. The flag was adopted in 1848. The civil ensign, known since 1911, was adopted in 1941 for use on the Rhine.

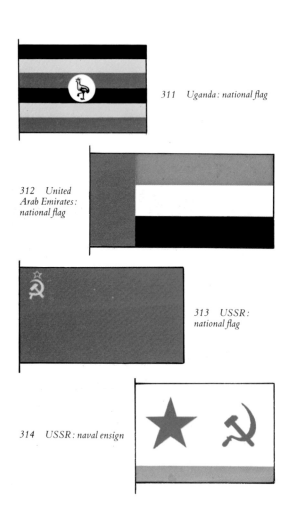

311 Uganda: national flag

312 United Arab Emirates: national flag

313 USSR: national flag

314 USSR: naval ensign

315   Russian SFSR

316
Armenian SSR

317   Azerbaidzhan
SSR

318   Byelorussian
SSR

159

It is like the national flag but with the ratio 2:3 as opposed to 1:1. Every city, commune, and canton of Switzerland has its own arms and flag. The flags are usually square banners of the arms.

Syria Syria joined the Federation of Arab Republics in January 1972, and adopted the common flag referred to under Egypt (p. 100). However, in April 1980 she reverted to the flag used prior to the Federation, which has two green stars on the central white band. The national emblem has also been altered.

Taiwan See China p. 92.

Tanzania Tanzania is an amalgamation of Tanganyika and Zanzibar, formed in April 1964. The flag of Tanganyika was originally green, black, green, horizontally, with yellow fimbriation, and dated from independence in December 1961. The present design includes a blue portion representing Zanzibar. This is taken from the blue, black, and green flag of Zanzibar.

Thailand The traditional emblem of Thailand is a white elephant on red, which provides two of the colours of the *Trairanga*, or tricolour, as the national flag is called. The blue was added in 1917 to symbolize solidarity with Allies. The white elephant, in caparisoned form, still appears in the centre of the naval ensign.

Syria: national emblem

The royal standard is charged with the *Garuda* in red on royal yellow. The *Garuda* is a mythical bird which features in Buddhist and Hindu mythology, and also appears in the arms of Indonesia. The flag of a royal prince is a blue square with the *Garuda* on a yellow disc in the centre.

The jack is like the national flag but has the naval emblem over all in the centre in yellow. This consists of an anchor passing through a *chakra* and ensigned by a Siamese helmet. The *chakra* is cognate with the one in the flag of India (see p. 117). The flag of an Admiral of the Fleet is a blue square with five white *chakras* around a device of crossed artillery shells and a wreath. Lesser admirals have only the *chakras*, in number according to their rank. Thailand has a very wide range of flags for the services and government departments.

Togo　The colours of Togo are the Pan-African colours first used by Ghana (p. 112). This flag was adopted on independence in April 1960 but was inspired by one used under the French administration. 305

Tonga　The flag of Tonga is the same now as it was when the islands became a British Protectorate. It was adopted in 1875, with the proviso that it should never be altered, and it was retained when the country regained its independence in June 1970. It signifies the Methodist persuasion of the inhabitants. There is a royal standard, also dating from 1875. This is a banner of the royal arms. 306

Trinidad and Tobago　The flag was adopted on independence in August 1962. The civil ensign has the ratio 1:2 and the national flag the ratio 3:5. The colours are taken from the coat of arms. The royal flag, used until the country became a republic in October 1976, was a banner of the arms with Queen Elizabeth's cypher in the centre. The naval ensign is like that of the UK (p. 36) but with the national flag, fimbriated white, in the canton. 307

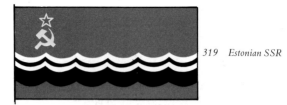

319   Estonian SSR

320   Georgian SSR

321   Kazakh SSR

322   Kirghiz SSR

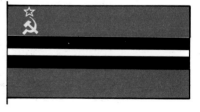

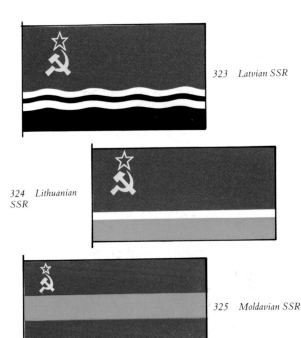

323 Latvian SSR

324 Lithuanian SSR

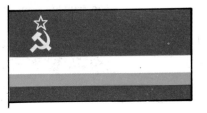

325 Moldavian SSR

326 Tadzhik SSR

308 **Tunisia**   The flag of Tunisia was adopted in 1835, prior to the French occupation, and was retained on independence in March 1956. Tunisia became a republic in July 1957, and the Bey's standard became obsolete. The crescent and star and the red and white colours are taken from the flag of Turkey, to which Tunisia once belonged.

309 **Turkey**   The crescent and star on the flag of Turkey have been explained in many different ways, none very satisfactory. The crescent has appeared on Turkish flags for many centuries, but the star was only added in the early nineteenth century. The flag was regularized towards the end of the last century, and was retained when the Ottoman Empire became the Republic of Turkey in October 1923.

The President's flag is a square version of the national flag with a gold device in the upper hoist.

Tuvalu   Formerly the Ellice Islands, Tuvalu was established as a separate British colony in October 1975, and became independent on 1 October 1978. The flag adopted on inde-
310 pendence has a light blue field with nine gold stars scattered over the fly, representing the nine islands of the group. In the canton is the Union Jack. There is also a coat of arms, granted in 1976, which appeared on the previous Blue Ensign.

311 **Uganda**   The emblem in the centre of the flag of Uganda is the African Balearic Crane, which was formerly the ensign-badge. It was also the badge of the dominant political party at the time of independence in October 1962. The colours too are those of the then dominant party.

The President's flag is red with the colours in narrow stripes along the lower edge, and the whole arms in the centre.

United Arab Emirates   The colours of the UAE are those
312 common to most Arab countries. The flag was adopted on independence in December 1971. Each of the seven members

164

has its own arms and flag. The flags of the various emirates are all red and white, originating in the treaty of 1820.

Union of Soviet Socialist Republics   The red flag appeared again in the revolution of 1917, having been used by revolutionaries on several previous occasions. It is said to have its origin in the Red Flag used by the Paris mob in the French Revolution. The red star was used by the Bolsheviks and by the Red Army, and so found a place in the new national flag in 313 November 1923, along with the hammer and sickle representing industrial and agricultural workers. The basic design of the flag has remained unchanged since 1923, but regulations of 1980 permit the omission of the hammer, sickle, and star from the reverse side. This is also true of the flags of the constituent republics.

The jack of the Soviet Navy is red, with the red star fimbriated white and charged with the hammer and sickle. The naval ensign is white with a light blue strip along the lower edge, and the red star and the hammer and sickle in large 314 proportions on the white field.

The Soviet Union is a federation of fifteen constituent republics, each with its own arms and flag. The largest republic, and the core of the Soviet Union, is the Russian Soviet Federal Socialist Republic. Its flag is like that of the USSR but with a 315 blue vertical strip in the hoist. This was adopted in January 1954, replacing the original Soviet Russian flag. Each autonomous republic also had its own arms and flag, but these are only variations of the emblems of the RSFSR itself.

The dates in the right-hand column below are the dates of introduction of the flags of the other constituent republics. These are all replacements of earlier designs. The flags of Byelorussia and the Ukraine were adopted as a result of their separate membership of the United Nations. The dates in the central column refer to the establishment of the constituent states as Soviet Socialist Republics. Several of them, e.g. the

327 Turkmen SSR

328 Ukraine SSR

329 Uzbek SSR

330 Uruguay: national flag and civil and naval ensign

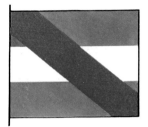

331 Uruguay : jack

332 Vanuatu : national flag

333 Vatican City State

334 Venezuela : national flag and civil ensign

Baltic states, existed as separate, often non-Communist, republics for a period after the fall of the Russian Empire.

Republic	Date of Establishment	Present Flag Adopted
316 Armenian SSR	29 November 1920	17 December 1952
317 Azerbaidzhan SSR	28 April 1920	18 August 1953
318 Byelorussian SSR	1 January 1919	25 December 1951
319 Estonian SSR	6 August 1940	6 February 1953
320 Georgian SSR	25 February 1921	11 April 1951
321 Kazakh SSR	5 December 1936	24 January 1953
322 Kirghiz SSR	5 December 1936	22 December 1952
323 Latvian SSR	5 August 1940	17 January 1953
324 Lithuanian SSR	3 August 1940	15 July 1953
325 Moldavian SSR	2 August 1940	31 January 1952
326 Tadzhik SSR	5 December 1929	20 March 1953
327 Turkmen SSR	27 October 1924	1 August 1953
328 Ukraine SSR	27 December 1917	21 November 1949
329 Uzbek SSR	27 October 1924	29 August 1952

330 **Uruguay**   The 'Sun of May' on the flag of Uruguay is like that on the flag of Argentina, to which country Uruguay once belonged. Independence was achieved in July 1828, and a flag of nineteen blue and white stripes was then adopted. These were
331 reduced to nine in July 1830. The jack is the flag of José Artigas, dating from April 1815, when he made the first attempt to free Uruguay from foreign rule.

The President's flag is white with the whole arms in the centre.

332 **Vanuatu**   The former New Hebrides, previously ruled jointly by Britain and France, became independent under this name in July 1980. The new national flag is in the colours of the dominant political party, and includes a well-known local emblem, a boar's tusk, containing two crossed fern leaves, symbolic of the traditional way of life.

Vatican City State   This flag was formerly the civil ensign 333 of the Papal States, suppressed in 1870, but resurrected in minuscule form in June 1929. The keys are the emblems of St Peter, and the colours of the flag are derived from them.

Venezuela   The colours of Venezuela are derived from the 334 flag introduced by Francisco de Miranda in 1806 in the first campaign to free South America from Spain. The seven stars stand for the seven original provinces. The State flag has the national arms in the canton; these were adopted in 1836, after secession from Greater Colombia. The President's flag is a square version of the national flag, with the arms over all in the centre and a white star at the centre of each side.

Vietnam   This flag dates from the 1940s, when left-wing 335 nationalists first began to struggle for independence. It became the flag of the state established in September 1945 in the north. The Communists gradually won control of the whole country, the final victory being in April 1975, after which the flag became that of a united Vietnam.

Western Samoa   The flag was first adopted in 1948, and 336 amended in February 1949, when Western Samoa was under the administration of New Zealand, on behalf of the United Nations. It was retained when the islands became independent in January 1962. The stars are those of the Southern Cross, and the general design recalls early flags of Samoa.

Yemen Arab Republic   The flag is based on that of the 337 former United Arab Republic, and dates from September 1962. The colours are the Pan-Arab colours of red, white, black and green (see p. 12).

Yemen People's Democratic Republic   This state is the former Aden colony and protectorate. The nationalists who won its independence made use of the Arab liberation colours (see Egypt p. 100), which were incorporated into the new 338

335 Vietnam:
national flag

336 Western
Samoa: national
flag and civil
ensign

337 Yemen Arab Republic:
national flag

338 Yemen People's Democratic
Republic: national flag

339 Yugoslavia: civil ensign

340 Yugoslavia: President

341 Bosnia-Herzegovina

342 Croatia

national flag, adopted in November 1967. The President's flag is the national flag with the state arms in the canton.

Yugoslavia Red, white and blue have been used in Yugoslavia since the colours were first adopted by Serbia in 1804, which borrowed them from the Russian flag. In 1918, when Yugoslavia was formed, they were placed in their present order. In January 1946 the red star, the emblem of Tito's partisans, was placed on the flag. The national flag is long, i.e. in the ratio 339 1:2, and the civil ensign short (2:3), the reverse of the usual practice.

340   The President's flag is square, with the national arms in the centre. The arms have six torches, representing the six constituent republics. The date is that of the proclamation of the republic. The naval ensign is red with the national flag in the canton, fimbriated white and with the red star surrounded by a gold wreath.

Each of the constituent republics has its own flag and emblem. Those of Croatia, Montenegro, Serbia, and Slovenia are old designs with the red star added. In the autonomous region of **Kosovo** the flag of Albania is used. The present designs of the constituent republic flags were adopted as follows:

341	Bosnia-Herzegovina	31 December 1946
342	Croatia	18 January 1947
343	Macedonia	31 December 1946
344	Montenegro	31 December 1946
344	Serbia	17 January 1947
345	Slovenia	16 January 1947

346 **Zaire** The present design was adopted in November 1971, and is the third national flag since the then Belgian Congo became independent in June 1960. It is based on the flag of the governing party, which shows a hand grasping a torch. It is also in the Pan-African colours.

347 **Zambia** The flag of Zambia was adopted on independence in October 1964. The colours are based on those of the ruling

party, although in an unusual and striking design. The President's flag is orange with the whole arms in the centre. The orange in the flags represents copper, the country's main mineral resource.

Zimbabwe   The legal independence of what was once 348 Rhodesia was achieved on 18 April 1980, after a brief return to British rule. The country is named after an ancient African city where the 'Zimbabwe Bird' was found. This featured on previous flags, and is now placed on the red star of socialism in the hoist of the new flag. This is striped in the colours of the ruling Zimbabwe African National Union. The Zimbabwe Bird and the red star are also the crest of the new coat of arms, and form a sort of national badge.

The President's Standard is green with the whole arms in the centre. In the hoist is a white triangle containing the red star and Zimbabwe bird, and in each fly canton are stripes of red, yellow, black, yellow, red—the ZANU colours.

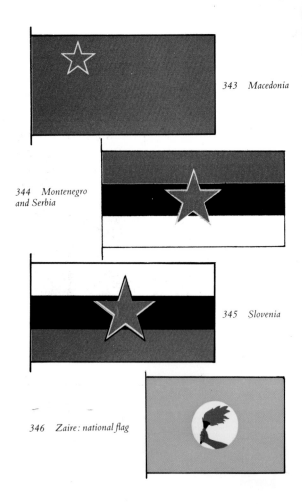

343 *Macedonia*

344 *Montenegro*
and Serbia

345 *Slovenia*

346 *Zaire: national flag*

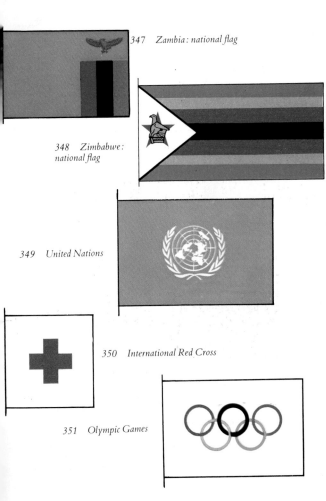

347   Zambia: national flag

348   Zimbabwe:
national flag

349   United Nations

350   International Red Cross

351   Olympic Games

175

INTERNATIONAL FLAGS

There are a large number of flags used internationally, on a world-wide scale, by inter-governmental organizations, defensive and economic alliances, religious groups, political and cultural movements, and other bodies of all kinds and purposes. The following is a very short selection of the many that could be presented.

United Nations   Outstanding among them all is the flag of the United Nations, officially adopted on 29 October 1947. It is in the colour now known as 'United Nations Blue', and the flag bears the UN emblem in white. This is a map of the world projected from above the North Pole, surrounded by olive branches of peace. The flag is flown all over the world on United Nations Day, 24 October, and in times of conflict by UN forces and observers.

International Red Cross   In 1869 in Switzerland, the countries of the Geneva Convention decided to use the flag of Switzerland with the colours reversed, to mark hospitals and medical personnel in time of war. The Red Cross has thereby become the best-known international badge. Equivalent flags have been adopted for Moslem countries (the Red Crescent), Israel (Red Shield of David) and the Soviet Union (Red Cross and Crescent).

Olympic Games   Perhaps the best-known of all international flags, this dates from 1913. The original flag, known as the standard, is carried from one Games to another. The five interlaced rings of different colours represent the five continents.

North Atlantic Treaty Organization   The NATO flag dates from October 1953. It is a compass rose within a ring and

349

350

351

352

four rays, all in white on a blue ground, representing the Atlantic Ocean.

Europe   Europe has no flag, although a great many international organizations within the continent have flags. The EEC, or Common Market, does not have a flag, although frequent attempts are made to find one. It is necessary to avoid the mistake made in the early Stars and Stripes, of having a design which must be altered with every new member, and also necessary to avoid a predominance of the colours of any one set of countries, difficulties which have not yet been overcome.

    The **Council of Europe** uses a flag adopted in September 353 1953. This at first was to have one gold star for each member, but the stars were restricted to twelve in 1955 to avoid constant changes. This is the flag most frequently thought of as the flag of 'Europe'.

Africa   There is a flag for the **Organization of African** 354 **Unity**, adopted about 1965. This has the badge of the organization in the centre, and colours which are not like those of any member country.

America   The best-known international flag in America is the **Flag of the Race**, i.e. the Hispanic race. This shows three 355 crosses like those on medieval Portuguese flags, representing the ships of Columbus, and a setting sun in gold representing the West. This flag is widely flown in Latin America on the Day of the Race, 12 October. It was designed by a Uruguayan in 1932.

Asia   There is no distinctively Asian flag, but one very widely used, especially in south and south-east Asia, is the international **Buddhist flag**, even though it is of American origin.   356

Fédération Internationale des Associations Vexillologiques   One of the newest cultural organizations to

352   North Atlantic
Treaty Organization

353   Council of Europe

354   Organization
of African Unity

355   Flag of the Race

356   Buddhist flag

357   Fédération Internationale
des Associations Vexillologiques

357 adopt an international flag is the FIAV. This flag was adopted in September 1967, and represents flag-halyards against the blue sky—the same blue as the UN flag. It is flown every two years at the International Congresses of Vexillology, when flag-enthusiasts from all over the world gather together.

SUGGESTIONS
FOR FURTHER READING

Flags of the World, E. M. C. Barraclough and W. G. Crampton, Frederick Warne, 1981

Flags and Arms Across the World, Whitney Smith, Cassell, 1980

Guide to Flags of the World, Whitney Smith, Sidgwick and Jackson, 1982

Flags, A Kingfisher Guide, Eric Inglefield, Kingfisher Books, 1986

Military Flags of the World 1618–1900, T. Wise, Blandford Press, 1977

Flags of All Nations, Ministry of Defence (Navy), HMSO, in volumes 1955 and 1958, with supplements

Flags of All Nations, Wall-chart, Brown Son & Ferguson, Glasgow, 1979

Flags at Sea, Timothy Wilson, HMSO, 1986

To keep up to date with flag changes and for features and articles on flag research, readers are recommended to subscribe to *Flagmaster*, the quarterly journal of the Flag Institute. Enquiries should be addressed to The Director, The Flag Institute, 10 Vicarage Road, Chester CH2 3HZ, England.

INDEX

Page numbers in **bold type** refer to colour illustrations.